UPS AND DOWNS

UPS AND DOWNS

Kathryn McCullough

KMC Publishing
Somewhere in Oregon

In my wildest dreams,
I never imagined being a 747 pilot.

ON THE RUNWAY

In 1981, I became Northwest Airline's fourth female pilot. I retired twenty-six years later as a Boeing 747 captain after an amazing roller coaster ride.

I would never have wanted to be an early settler or pioneer. Exploring is fun, but hacking westward on the Oregon Trail would not have been my lifestyle choice. Thankfully, I didn't realize I was an aviation pioneer. I became a pilot because I loved to fly.

On the one hand I was a star. Every time I walked into the cockpit, one of the pilots would say, "Wow! I've never flown with a female pilot before!" Men gaped as I walked down the concourse in my uniform. Women stopped to praise me and to thank me for being in such a tough career, paving the way. Parents told their little girls, "Look, a female pilot. You could be a pilot!"

On the flip side, I was a necessary evil. Each time I walked onto an airplane I was starting from scratch. I had to prove I could fly. Military pilots I flew with told me I should be home raising my family, and no, they weren't joking. Women were nervous about a female flying their plane. Japanese men deplaned if they saw me in the cockpit. Male passengers stopped to give me flying lessons or to criticize the landing, even if it was the captain's landing.

My life has been exciting and full. I've been to places I had only dreamed of. I've scaled mountains I never thought of climbing.

What is the one thing I would change?
I would relax more and enjoy the ride.

The most important people in my life:
My husband Kevin with our daughter, Darcie, and son, Colton.

Twenty-five years of service with Northwest Airlines...what a ride!

WHAT IT TAKES

There is always a recipe that goes with baking a great cake. Certain ingredients are required for a wonderful life, too.

My core ingredients were standard: determination, tenacity, courage, common sense, and a huge dose of faith. I wasn't born rich, but I always had a roof over my head and food on the table. I wasn't a straight-A student, but I got good grades. Love, encouragement, and support from family and friends were invaluable.

Honesty and integrity are most important to me. I strived to be a good wife and mother, as well as a safe pilot with no accidents and a good reputation. I'm strong and virtually unbreakable. Having a good attitude and never giving up helped more than I imagined.

Traveling, writing, speaking, and being a photographer are the icing on my cake. There isn't enough room on this page, but by the end of the book you will see why I love my life.

Just like there are thousands of cake recipes, there are a multitude of 'life' recipes. What's yours?

You can read this book straight through, or jump around.
Chronologically, it is in order.
Most of the chapters stand alone.

Granddaddy Bice reading to me.

Our little white house in Dover, Delaware.

PEOPLE MATTER

My childhood was idyllic. I was two years older than my brother, Jim. We lived in a small white house with a yard that backed up to a soybean field. There was a swing set in the backyard, and a safe street in front. We knew all our neighbors. My parents didn't want us calling adults by their first names, so we prefaced their friend's names by aunt or uncle. Aunt Sarah and Uncle Larry lived on one side, and Aunt Gladys and Uncle Joe were on the other, with Aunt Jane and Uncle Bill two houses down. I grew up surrounded by a *huge* family.

I had the best grandfather in the world. He was the kindest, most caring man I've ever known. I spent Tuesdays and Thursdays at my paternal grandparent's house when I was young. Nana was a worrier, who stayed home. Granddaddy never knew a stranger, and we walked hand in hand to the cigar store for candy, saying hello to everyone we met.

Dover, Delaware's main street was busy and filled with cars in the late fifties. Drivers honked angrily and pedestrians yelled at the Amish slowing down traffic in their horse-drawn buggies. Not Grandaddy. He stopped to help the Amish men tie up their buggies, and he leant a hand to help the women step down. He greeted them warmly, like long-lost friends.

My grandfather taught me to value the differences in people instead of judging them harshly. He died in his sleep when I was six. Jim and I would open Grandaddy's pipe caddy and cigar box, inhaling the scent to remember him. There was a huge hole in our lives.

Our dad grew up in Dover, and most of his friends and family still lived there. He knew everyone in town, it seemed, and everyone knew him. He had a way of making people feel at ease, like his father. Having a firm foundation of love and friendships was a huge building block in my life.

We went to Rehoboth Beach every summer with Dad's best friend, Alden Richardson. Uncle Alden and Aunt Becky had a three-story house by the boardwalk. An original log cabin sat beside it. Dad seemed to know everyone in Rehoboth, too. The Richardson kids were about our age, and oh, the fun we would have! Our imaginations ran wild playing house in the log cabin and exploring the attic of the huge house.

Every day was beach day, and if it were up to us, we would never have got out of the water. Our parents lured us with Fireball candies, a great excuse for a break. We weren't allowed to bite the Fireball, just suck on it. It was so hot that we took it out of our mouths every few seconds, laughing and sitting on our towels, resting before jumping more waves.

Evenings were spent building forts under the boardwalk, or climbing on overturned lifeguard chairs and searching the sand for leftover treasures of the day: buckets and toys, tanning lotion and shells. We loved the high, unfinished end of the boardwalk, and would run towards it, flying into the sand piles below. We played while our parents played Monopoly and put together jigsaw puzzles, laughing and talking late into the night. Once a week we would go into town for saltwater taffy, ride the bumper cars, and jump on the trampolines.

I've always been friendly—"dangerously friendly" my mother would say. A few years ago we were visiting Uncle Alden and Aunt

Becky. When Mom complained about me being too friendly to Uncle Alden, he looked at me and said, "Well you're just like your dad and granddad, aren't you?" The light bulb came on and I realized I should be proud of being friendly... I came by it honestly.

Seeing the best in people goes a long way in this world.

My 4th grade class photo in Indiana. I'm in the middle row, third from right...
I can remember my friends but not their names.

My brother and me at Rehoboth Beach in the 1950s.

The Richardson kids, Sally and Brad, with us!

DETERMINATION

I was stubborn and headstrong as a little girl. I could scream for hours after being sent to my room. My mother was afraid the neighbors would call the police on her for child abuse, even though I was never beaten and rarely spanked. I just wouldn't back down. Mom always apologized to *me* after I cried and cried. We battled endlessly.

I remember my parents insisted we try a bite of everything on our plates at dinner. My brother Jim and I hated lima beans. Every time we had lima beans, it was a test of wills. Jim was smart. He would pretend to eat the bite, holding the beans in his cheek until going to the bathroom to spit them out. Not me. I had to fight with our parents. One night, Dad told me that if I didn't eat that one bite he would break my favorite record. I was the boss. I never gave in. I knew Dad wouldn't break my record. I was wrong.

Dad went upstairs, found my favorite record, and snapped my little yellow 45 in half over his knee. I didn't want my dad to know he had bested me. Screaming, I ran upstairs like a crazy person and returned with a record that looked identical to my favorite. "Ha ha. You got the wrong one," I screeched as I ran to hide it.

Maybe a good paddling would have helped.

What I didn't know was that my father had leukemia and was dying. Mom and Dad kept it a secret for six years, even from his parents. I think they were both afraid. There was underlying turmoil in our house, and, in fairness, I was probably reacting to it.

My father was always sick. He caught every cold or flu going around, and his mom, my Nana, was always after him to wear a heavier coat, scarf, hat, and mittens. My brother and I spent summers with my mom's parents in Indiana while Dad went to Johns Hopkins Medical Center in Baltimore for treatments. My brother and I never knew why we really went to see our grandparents, and we never knew how sick he was.

Stubborn and determined, that's me.

My tantrums stopped when my dad died. I cried myself to sleep every night for the rest of the year. Our family was broken. Maybe my life wasn't so idyllic. We missed him so much.

***Determination is a good thing. No matter how bad
the weather or circumstances, I never quit.
And I don't cry, although sometimes I wish I could.***

LITTLE THINGS ADD UP

How do I not remember more about my father? It baffles me. He was such a big part of my life when I was little. I do remember some things… like him tucking me in at night, "tight or loose?" and making sure my closet door was closed, because I thought there might be monsters in there. My cat had been spayed after having kittens, so we took her to the beach with us, all bandaged up. I kept a good eye on her, but she got out of the house. I saw her three doors down, weaving back and forth between the legs of a Great Dane. I started crying, panicked that she was going to be killed and eaten! My dad bent down beside me and told me to watch, not worry. "Animals are smart. She knows he's a friend, see how she's rubbing against his legs? See?"

Another time I came home from school talking about my new art teacher with a fat leg. Dad didn't scold me for making fun of her. He took me on his lap and told me he grew up with my teacher, how nice she was, and that her leg used to be pretty. "She went to Africa to help people and was bitten by a mosquito that carried a disease." He told me to tell her hello from him.

We had a huge neighborhood Halloween party the year he died. It was one of Dad's last "wishes." Our basement was filled with trashcans full of popcorn, tubs of water with apples for bobbing, and apples and marshmallows on strings hanging from the ceiling for games. Dad made up a scary story about the Itchy Gitchy Goomy Tree in Porter's front yard. We walked all the neighborhood kids home that night, and I remember Mrs. Porter thanking him so much; now her girls were going to be afraid to walk up to their own house! She and my dad were good friends, and when he died four months later, she had me over to her house to sew clothes for my Barbie. The kindness and support we received from all his friends and family helped us heal.

I learned at church that God answers prayers. I was praying as hard as I could for God to bring my dad back, but he wasn't answering. I remember being so angry that I stopped praying. My Sunday school teacher realized what was going on, and told me that God always listened, but prayers wouldn't all be answered in the way we hoped. Now my faith helps me through everything in my life.

I worried that Dad's memories of me would be of what a brat I was. Thank goodness I talked to my Uncle Alden. He said my father was so proud of me and that he would always say, "I never worry about Kathy. My Kathy can do anything in this world."

Having someone like my dad in my life, someone who believed in me so much, how could I not succeed?

Nice is not a four letter word.

Daddy washing my feet.

LOVE AND MONEY

I wasn't born rich. My father wasn't a pilot. He was a loan officer at a bank and a volunteer fireman. I was eight-years-old when he died. My mother had a tough time supporting us on her salary of $7,000 a year. "If you really love your children," she told me, "you have to be able to support them." Mom decided to go back for a Master's Degree at Northwestern University.

My brother and I were overjoyed. We would be living with our grandparents in their beautiful house on the St. Joseph River in Osceola, Indiana. Our idyllic summers would last all year.

My maternal grandparents, aunts, uncles, and cousins were the best family I could have hoped for. Picnics by the river, family reunions, challenging croquet games, catching lightening bugs, boating—we did it all. I had a vivid imagination, and with our new friends, we built forts and played make believe for hours after school. You can't underestimate the power of love. Grandpa and Grandma helped us turn the corner on our grief.

When we moved back to Delaware, my brother and I had a new awareness of what it took to keep a family together. We knew Mom worked hard to support us, and we tried to help her, too. Losing our father was hard, but we learned how to treasure his memory and make the best of life without him.

I knew for a fact that money didn't grow on trees. Watching my mom, I learned that you never give up, no matter how hard things get.

My parents knew Dad had leukemia when this picture was taken.
The outlook was grim.

My poor cat put up with a lot from me.

INTEGRITY

I went to fourth grade in Indiana and made friends quickly at my new school. On the first day a group of kids took me in, and we spent recess talking and getting to know each other. The only problem was that some of the kids were tagging the playground equipment. I found myself in the principal's office.

I was so embarrassed. My grandparents were such good people, and I hated to disappoint them. My grandmother came to get me, and the look of shame on her face cut me to the core. My punishment was to sand and grind the writing off. "But I didn't do it. I was just talking while some of the kids did it."

"You were there. You knew what they were doing was wrong. You are as guilty as they are," my grandparents said.

That is a lesson I've never forgotten. It took a week to clean up the playground, and we had to paint the benches and pick up trash. After that week, I never hung around that group of kids again. I found good friends—friends with values that matched mine.

Now, if I'm someplace a wrong is being committed, I stop the behavior if I can or protest with my feet by walking away. I don't want to be around people who don't treat others well, and I don't want to be around anyone who doesn't have integrity. I'm always looking in the mirror, questioning my actions and trying to do the right thing.

I'm always falling short of being my best self,
but I keep trying.

Friends in Indiana.

Cousins in Indiana

BRAVERY

Mom remarried and we moved to Florida the summer after fifth grade. I missed my old friends, but I made new ones. The whole idea in our new neighborhood was to be tough. My initiation into the local "gang" was walking on sharp gravel and hot asphalt in bare feet without wincing or crying out. I didn't have tough Florida-feet like they did, but I wasn't about to let them see me fail. So I gritted my teeth and did it. Once I proved myself, I was in.

My new friends showed me where to find shark's teeth in the creeks and Indian arrowheads in the fields. They knew the locations of sinkholes and secret ponds, as well as showing me huge live oak trees to climb and abandoned houses to explore. We played hide and seek on horseback and swam to our heart's content. The new experiences and friends were great. But there was also a neighborhood bully named Tom.

Tom was bigger than I was, but not by much. I was older, but only by a grade—I was in sixth and he was in fifth. Everyone was terrified of him, and he ruled the street with an iron fist. We usually avoided him, and I wasn't ever on the receiving end of his attacks, but many of the littler kids were. His mistake was picking on my dog.

My new dad had a German wire-haired pointer named Gabby. Gabby had been Dad's savior when he was recovering from polio. When Dad came back from the Korean War to his young wife and son, he was no longer the strong, handsome, and whole man she had married. He was bedridden and unable to walk. Dad's wife went to the bars and found love, just like the old Kenny Roger's song, "Ruby Don't Take Your Love to Town."

One day, Dad's wife left him, but she left their two-year-old son, Keith, with him. Dad's mom moved in to help them. Two years later, just as Dad was able to claim desertion and get full custody, his wife came back and disappeared with their son. He was heartbroken.

Gabby saw my dad through the hardest times in his life, and we loved our dog, too. Now Gabby was getting mean. He was nice to us, his adopted kids. And he was nice to friends we brought home. But he was vicious to kids on the other side of the fence, and we couldn't figure out why. We were afraid that he might have to be put down, and Dad was the most afraid of all.

When I caught Tom torturing my dog, teasing and provoking him, it all made sense. I flew into a rage and challenged him to a fight. Laughing, he told me to "bring it on." I did. With all the neighbor kids gathered on the fence, rooting for me, I had Tom down within minutes. I was sitting on his stomach, Queen of the World. Every time Tom tried to get up, I would bounce. And call him Tommy. Humiliated, he promised to stop picking on little kids and my dog.

But when I let him up, he jumped me from behind. I was afraid the first time had just been luck, until I got him down again. And again. I think I was still mad about Gabby. The third time I had had it. I bounced harder. I was afraid I might have hurt his stomach. The kids cheered louder. It didn't feel that great to me this time, and I started wondering what it would take to teach this kid a lesson. I made him promise, again. He finally started crying, and I let him up. He ran for home.

Believe it or not, Tommy stopped bullying. But the other kids were now out for retaliation. I didn't want to break Tom's spirit— I just wanted him to stop bullying. Tom's family moved away. I always wondered if he learned his lesson, or if I just created a monster. I guess I'll never know. But Gabby got better, and we kept him.

I spent the next six years exploring Florida's creeks, ponds, and woods. When we moved across town the next year, I became a bit of a loner. I found a new favorite reading spot a mile from our house, high up in an old oak tree which sprawled over a pond. There were alligators, water snakes, skinks, giant spiders, lizards, and other creeping, crawling things. Poisonous snakes were everywhere: moccasins, rattlers, and corals.

I was safe up in my tree. The branches were fat and more comfortable than a chair when you leaned back against the giant trunk. Spanish moss dripped all around, and the pond reflected a sky full of beautiful cotton ball clouds beneath me. It was a safe cocoon in a foreign world.

One afternoon after hours of reading, I heard strange, grunting noises beneath me. Looking down, I saw three alligators. They were small—about five feet long, but they were close to my tree. Walking home from school a few weeks before, I'd seen an alligator chase our neighbor's dog around their house three *times*. The little dog was running flat out, and the alligator was up on its stubby legs keeping up! I wasn't that fast. I knew I couldn't outrun them. I had to out-wait them.

I kept reading my book, looking down every few minutes. Half an hour later they were still there. An hour later it was starting to get dark. The gators didn't know I was above them, but it seemed like they were waiting. For dinner.

Could I find my way home in the dark? I sure didn't want to. There were too many twists and turns, too many pitfalls and sinkholes. I didn't want to spend the night in the tree, either. Did Florida snakes live in trees? I knew there were possums and panthers and all kinds of night animals that did. I worried, but the lesser evil seemed to be to stay put. By some miracle, the next time I looked down, they were gone.

Quickly I shinnied down the furthest branch from the pond, just in case they were still nearby. I jumped to the ground, praying I didn't jump on anything alive... like the coiled rattlesnake that was there last week. I ran as fast as I could in the darkening woods, crashing through spider webs and bushes. If there were any animals around, I'm sure I scared them away. Finally, I saw the lights of home.

Breathlessly I ran into our house. I could hear silverware clanking in the dining room. I was so late that everyone was eating dinner—dinner that I was supposed to help make. I knew I was in trouble. Mom and Dad were furious.

I told them what had happened, but by the looks on their faces I knew they didn't believe me. My brother snickered. No one believed me. I was sent to my room without dinner for being late and for lying. I was glad to be home, with all my limbs attached, and my rumbling stomach was a small price to pay.

Never panic.

MATH

As sixth grade wound down, my teacher told my mom I was doing poorly in math. We still visited our grandparents in the summer, and Mom told them I would have to take remedial math. In five years I had attended five schools: Dover Elementary, Elsie Rogers in Indiana, back to Dover, Stephen Foster in Florida, and now Westwood.

My grandfather decided I must have missed some basic skills in all our moving around. Grandpa came home the next day with a huge stack of math workbooks. I scoffed at him because the first and second grade ones in the pile were so easy. He told me he paid a penny a page.

I whizzed through the first book in minutes, and the next five almost as fast. Then I slowed down. As the books became harder, Grandpa upped the pay to a nickel a page. Watching my progress, he could tell when I was slowing down or getting discouraged. He upped each page to a dime, and finally a quarter, helping me at night when I got stuck. By the end of the summer, I was rich. I also tested into Accelerated Math at my new school. I remember my newfound confidence—standing at the blackboard, chalk in hand, working out complicated problems for Mr. McGill. On my tests, I got As. *And it seemed easy.*

You can't be a very good pilot without common sense, logical thinking, and math skills. To this day, I love math, calculus, algebra, statistics, and geometry. Logic puzzles and brainteasers are fun. Thanks to my grandfather, I had the basics covered.

*You can learn anything
with the right tools and motivation.*

*My grandparents were kind and let us live with them in Indiana
while Mom went back to school.*

My grandparents' home in Indiana

GOOD NOT BAD

Snakes were a big part of living in Florida. I wasn't afraid of them—I just hadn't seen any snakes in Indiana or Delaware. We had a hognose snake in our sixth grade classroom. If we completed our work early, we could hold the snake or read from giant fairy tale books from around the world. I did both. The snake was fun, and he would puff up and hiss at you. Walking through the cow pasture near our new house was always an experience, because some of the cow patties moved when you stepped on them. Those were just black snakes. Good snakes.

But the snakes around my next house were not as harmless. We had a coral snake in the side yard, moccasins or cottonmouths down by the pond, and diamond back rattlesnakes everywhere. It wasn't scary… you just had to be vigilant. I was careful, but aware. I stomped loudly to vibrate the ground. I never had a problem, but I knew they were there.

I didn't know how many snakes there were until I was walking home from school one day. The prisoners were cleaning the culverts and mowing along Main Street where the bus dropped me off. I had my sandals on, and there were snake bodies everywhere in the cut grass. It was disgusting. And scary. There were huge heads and body parts to step around and over. I walked up the hill on Main Street, even with all the traffic. I didn't cut through the bushes to my yard, either. I stayed on the pavement. And I decided that I would never break the law or go to prison if that is what you had to do as punishment.

Every time the prisoners cleared the culverts, there were just as many snakes as before. They were everywhere. I just rarely saw them.

I didn't stop exploring or having fun in the woods. We still took our duck boat out on the pond for water lily fights. *Carefully.* I made even more noise than before, if that were possible. I never got bitten, or even came close. The most important lesson, for me, is that there is always danger lurking. The world is not a safe place. But you don't want to concentrate on the bad. There is too much good.

Concentrate on the good, not the bad.

The Bangkok snake farm.

FEAR

I wasn't afraid of much. I remember being dragged under by the ocean at Rehoboth Beach one time when I was little. I kept trying to get up, but the waves knocked me back down before I could get my breath. Around the sixth time or so, I was tired and ready to give up. I wasn't scared: I just couldn't do it anymore. Then I felt the strong arms of my father lift me up.

After my father died, I became afraid of little things. I'd always been afraid of the dark hole in my closet at night, and that's why I had him check inside, and then shut it, before I went to sleep. I had a vivid imagination, and I was sure I heard men in the attic crawl-space until my dad took me in there with a flashlight. Whatever I was afraid of, my Dad always reassured me. Now he was gone and my new fear was the dogs that barked all night long down the alley. I was sure they were wolves that ate small children.

Aunt Gladys was from Scotland, and her parents came to visit each year. Her mother was tiny and kind, with a bag of Scottish peppermints she passed out freely, but she didn't speak much English. Dan Dan, Aunt Gladys' father, was a tall man with a thick brogue who spoke English well and loved to walk. Of course he took me with him. I confided in him about the dogs. He took my hand and walked me down the alley. After months of being afraid, he showed me that the dogs were just... dogs. They were in kennels, and none of them looked like wolves. He told me they were just scared because their owners were on vacation and they were in a strange place. They barked, or talked, to each other so they wouldn't be as scared. But the biggest lesson for me was to confront my fears instead of being afraid.

Of course there is a time to be afraid and just run. I've done that, too. When I was fifteen, something happened that scared me more than anything else in my life. I was "church shopping," trying desperately to find a religion that spoke to me. I was raised Presbyterian, but I wanted more. I liked the Episcopalian religion because of the reverence—the kneeling, the red velvet, and the holiness of it all. The Baptists seemed too strict for me, I decided, after going with a Baptist girlfriend to her church. That summer I was in New England, working as a governess. I tried Quaker, Methodist, Lutheran—all the churches within walking distance of my employer's house in Wellesley, Massachusetts, on my Sundays off, and I enjoyed them all.

Now we were in the country in New Hampshire, and there was an Evangelist church down the road that I could walk to. It was in an old farmhouse, and they held their services on Tuesday evenings and Sunday mornings. The people were friendly, and I loved the singing. I could hardly wait for Sunday. I was getting the kids in bed on a Friday night when I noticed cars going down the street. There must be a special service they had forgotten to tell me about!

Once the kids were in bed, I told their grandmother I was going for a walk. By the time I got to the church, the yard was full of cars and the gate was closed. No one was around, as the service had already started. It was the first time I noticed the barbed wire on the white fence, and what looked like a guard shack near the entrance. I knew something was off. I should have turned around and gone home. Instead I slipped in and headed for the house.

Something stopped me before I got to the front door—probably the strange chanting. I went to the side of the church and stood on my tiptoes to look in a window. The place was packed. I recognized some of the people from the Evangelical services I went to. Everyone was dressed in black, hooded robes, chanting and swaying. At the front of the church, something was writhing on the altar. The leader had a huge knife, like a machete. I saw blood spurt up into the air as the blade came down. To this day, I can't tell you what else happened or what was killed up there, but I can tell you it scared the hell out of me. That's all I remember seeing before I turned and ran. Of course I never went back, although I was afraid someone might have seen me looking in. And I never told my employer or anyone else about the farmhouse until years later. I was afraid they would be angry and hurt the children. Besides, summer was almost over.

The thing that scared me the most was that the people I met seemed *nice*. How did I reconcile nice with devil worship? It was something that I couldn't figure out. But the biggest lesson, for me, was that evil is real—very real. To this day I stay away from people whose words and actions don't match my ideals—people who don't know right from wrong.

Know when to walk and know when to run.

Stephen and Molly, pictured with their aunt and uncle, were little sweethearts, and I felt more like their sister than their governess.

I loved playing games with kids and babysitting.

TENACITY

"There will be no breakfast until you finish your chores."

I rolled over and opened my eyes. My employer was standing over me, shaking her finger. Her hair was pulled back tightly, giving her a mini-facelift. Her no-nonsense shoes tapped angrily on the wooden floor.

What did I forget to do? I racked my brain. Yesterday the kids and I cleaned the guesthouse from top to bottom. The day before we sanded and painted the porch floor. The kids and I pretend she is our wicked stepmother who makes us work from sunup to sundown for our room and board. Although it is disrespectful, it helps us turn an unpleasant situation into a game. And it is not that far-fetched. She's mean. Stephen and Molly cry before and after their morning violin and German lessons with her. But we swim every afternoon at a swimming pool in a pasture on a hill. In spite of Grandmamma, we are still having a great summer.

I stayed up until eleven last night folding and ironing her clothes. Was that it? I didn't put them away? "Put away the clothes?" I ask.

She let out a pent up, bone weary sigh. "Oh, I do wish my husband were still alive. He was so much better with the help."

The help. That's me. Slave labor for a measly twenty-five dollars a week. I was hired to babysit her two grandchildren while their parents worked during the summer, and I flew with them from Gainesville to Boston. Last month, at her other house in Wellesley, we had a maid and a cook. Now, at the country house in New

Hampshire, it's just me. Luckily I can't cook or I'd probably be doing everything.

"Think. Is there something you forgot to do last night, something important?" She holds my gaze. Lips pursed, she tsks at me and cocks her head. I feel like a troublesome pet. Apparently I am hopelessly dense. I shake my head. She sighs again. "You forgot to iron my bra straps and my undergarments. You may eat after you finish your job. I'm sure someday you will be someone famous, but right now you are just hired help." Mrs. Schwartz did an about face and marched off.

Bra straps? Underwear? Ironed? Right. Why didn't I think of that? Grrr. I've thought about quitting, but I wouldn't. The empathy I have with the children goes way beyond being a governess. I am their protector and friend. *Wait, she thinks I'll be somebody famous?*

I toughed out the summer and earned a $100 bonus. Mrs. Schwartz was quite pleased with the way I "turned out," as she puts it. Thinking seriously about my future, I know I never want to be a governess again. What do I want to be? I want to be someone, and definitely not hired help. Maybe someone famous...

Even if it sucks, stick it out.

USE YOUR INNER COMPASS

I envy people who know their calling. One of my husband's cousins wanted to be a monk. At age six he was blessing people and giving funerals to dead animals. Now he is a brother in the Catholic Church. Another cousin was always checking out people's teeth as a child, and of course he's a dentist.

I wish I could say I knew what I wanted to do when I grew up. I knew I had to start somewhere. I thought about being an interior designer. I redecorated my room and read design magazines cover to cover, never throwing them away. Maybe I would be an architect. Frank Lloyd Wright must be related to my paternal grandmother whose maiden name was Wright. Maybe it was in my genes! I constructed a model of my ideal home—a ranch house with barns and sheds and chicken coops. I kept it on a table in my closet for years and told friends I was going to marry a Montana sheep rancher.

I knew what I didn't want. I hated cooking and I barely made it through Home Economics in the eleventh grade. Aviation and chemistry were my two choices for science electives as a senior. Friends told me chemistry was too much like cooking, so I took aviation. We were "guinea pigs" at the University of Florida's laboratory school, and aviation was an "experimental" subject. Dr. Gadsden, my physics professor, was teaching it, so I knew it would be a good class. We studied basic meteorology, aerodynamics, flight planning, and FAA rules and regulations—all that was necessary to pass the private pilot written test.

I told my parents I either wanted to learn to parachute or learn to fly. My mom had a friend who had broken his back three times skydiving. She invited him to dinner, hoping his stories and pain would convince me *not* to jump out of a perfectly good airplane. Mom succeeded. In fact, if that weren't enough, every time I went to an airport where there was skydiving going on, someone was taken away in a body bag or an ambulance. Flying was another story. The only pilot my mother knew worked for Braniff Airlines, and he loved his job. He wasn't invited to dinner.

My class went to the airport on a field trip, and most of the kids brought twenty dollars for an introductory flight. My money was in the bank, and since Mom didn't want to encourage me to fly, she wouldn't lend me the money. So, I stood on the ground watching as my friends took ride after ride. My classmates were thrilled when they came back from the wild blue yonder, going on and on about how fun it was. The instructor let them fly the plane, doing turns, climbs, and descents. What a blast!

I could only watch everyone else having fun for so long, so I went inside the building and made friends with the receptionists instead. We hit it off. They needed someone to work weekends and asked if I would be interested in the job. I would get twenty percent off flying lessons and supplies. Of course I said yes. I flew home on cloud nine.

My mother quickly nixed the idea. "You don't have a car and I need mine on the weekend." I had already solved that problem.

"One of the guys who works there pumping gas says he'll pick me up. He just lives a mile from us."

The first day Paul picked me up on his motorcycle, he handed me a purple helmet. I saw the curtains move in my parent's bedroom window as I climbed on, and I knew my mom was watching us. Sure enough, from then on, she let me borrow the car.

I worked thirty-two hours—two weekends—to afford a one-hour lesson. It was worth every minute. I could hardly wait for the two weeks to pass, but at least I was at the airport talking to pilots in between my lessons. Flying was exhilarating, and I was giddy with anticipation of each new lesson. I loved counting swimming pools. I wasn't the most serious student my instructor had because I didn't want to be a pilot for a living—I just wanted to be able to fly my friends to the beach for lunch. My instructor's comment in my logbook was that I needed to pay more attention to flying and stop sightseeing. So I did. That's when I decided I wanted to be a pilot.

You never get anywhere if you don't start down a path. You wander aimlessly, weaving like a snake in shifting sands, blaming others if your life isn't working out. Pick a path. You can always branch off, or change direction.

You don't always have to know where you are going as long as you're headed somewhere.

I didn't solo in a tail dragger, and this wasn't me. But anything can happen if you get care-less. The saying is, "There are those who have ground looped, and those who will."

Date 3-4-72	Course PRi		Lesson II		Student				
A/C make Cessna	Model 150		Horsepower 100		N# 60139		Grade		

| Flight Time | Total Time | | Cross Country | | Instrument | | | Night | | Ground |
	Dual	Solo	Dual	Solo	Actual	Hood	Trainer	Dual	Solo	Training
This flight	9	.3		2.3						
Previous	168		14							
Total	177		14	2.3						

Preflight Procedures	Rectangular Course	Forward Slip	Unfamiliar Airport Procedure	Emergency Go-arounds
Flight planning	"S" Turns	Side Slip	Radio: Comm. & Navigation	Short Field Landings
Use of Check Lists	Confidence Maneuvers	Emergency Descents	Radio Tuning	Soft Field Landings
Aircraft Pre-flight	Medium Turns	Hi Angle Climb, Turn Recvy	Radio Communications	Cross Wind Landings
Starting Engines	Ground Reference Maneuvers	Recovery / Unusual Attitudes	VOR Orientation	Accuracy Landings
Taxi and Takeoff Procedures	Normal Descents	Spiral Recovery	VOR Interception	Slips to a Landing
Taxiing	Altitude & Speed Control	8's On	VOR Tracking	Parking
Normal Takeoffs	Level off from Glides	8's Around	ADF	Servicing
Traffic Patterns	Speed Changes	720 Steep Turns (9 point)	DF	Night Flying
Climbs	Turns to Headings	Lazy 8's	DME	Use of Navigation Lights
Climbing Turns	Timed Turns	Spins	Radar	Landing Lights
Level Off	Standard Rate 360° Turns	Chandelles	Approach & Landg. Procedures	Airport Lighting
Aborted Takeoffs	Steep Turns	Cross Country Procedures	Traffic Pattern Entry	
Cross Wind Takeoffs	Glides & Gliding Turns	Cross Country Planning	Use of Flaps	
Short Field Takeoffs	Slow Flight	Flight Plans	180° Side Approach	
Soft Field Takeoffs	Descents at Min. Cont. Speed	Cross Country Flying	360° Gliding Approaches	
Max. Performance Takeoff	Power Off Stalls	Magnetic Compass	Normal Landings	Coordination
Maneuvers	Accelerated Stalls	Forced Landings	Full Stall Landings	Aptitude
Straight and Level	Cross Control Stalls	Lost Procedure	Power Approach	Planning
Shallow Turns	Stalls from Critical Attitudes	Cross Country Emergencies	Power Landing	Judgment

Remarks: Must stop sightseeing & start concentrating on learning to fly.

	Rate/Hr.	Dual	Solo
Time Flown	$	$	$
Total Charges	$		$

Above Instruction Given: Roy E Brown 798901 CFI

Above Instruction Received: Kathy Buce

COURAGE

Solo? Three landings alone? At sixteen years old?

What if I crash? Stupid thought. Troy, my instructor, would never let me go up alone if he thought I couldn't land a Cessna 150.

The plane seemed so empty. It flew differently. It was lighter without Troy, and it seemed to leap off the ground on takeoff. *Weird.* Shaking, I made the first two landings, a little clunky, floating a little, pretending Troy was in the other seat, encouraging me. On final approach for my third landing, the tower told me to make an immediate left turn. *This was new.* I shook my head, laughing to myself as I turned. My instructor must have called the tower controller, told him I was on my first solo flight, and asked him to test my ability to follow instructions. I circled and was re-cleared to land.

I greased the last landing on. Yes! My first, uneventful solo flight! Proudly I taxied in.

There was a large crowd of people waiting outside the flight school. *For me?* I taxied to a stop, went through my engine shut-down checklist, and hopped out, feeling like a rock star.

Everyone rushed towards me. "Are you okay? Are you all right? Were you scared?"

"No, I'm good. It was fun!" *I've seen guys solo and they never get this fanfare. It must be because I'm a girl.*

"But you're okay? That was so close! A near midair!"

A near what? I didn't have a clue what they were talking about. I looked at my instructor. Troy said an airplane without a radio entered the pattern above me. He cut me off, barely missing me by fifty feet or less! If I hadn't followed the tower's instructions as quickly as I did, I would be dead.

The tower called to apologize for the mishap. Apparently the pilot lost his radio, but saw the green traffic light on Waldo Road and thought the tower was clearing him to land! *Wow, I never even saw him.* Thank goodness Troy was such a good instructor and I did what I was told.

Cutting off my shirttail and signing my logbook were a blur. I soloed! At dinner that night I didn't tell my parents how close I came to dying. I just told them I soloed.

Being brave isn't always a choice.
Sometimes it's a surprise.

Seriously, would you trust your life to this teenager?

CHALLENGES

We all have challenges in life, and other people's circumstances seem so much worse than mine. I feel lucky to have had the chances and opportunities I've had. Dwelling on the bad is counterproductive.

Besides, I learn so much from my challenging experiences.

Being a governess, working at McDonald's, waitressing, pumping gas, washing airplanes, being a flight attendant, working as a health and safety inspector... all my jobs taught me valuable lessons and skills. I learned about people and I learned about the world. It took years to become an airline pilot, and that is the part that is tough sometimes.

Going inch-by-inch, step-by-step, is so hard when you are impatient and want it now. To me, it was the process that was fun, not just the end result. People always ask me if flying a 747 is difficult. They're surprised when I say no.

It would have been impossible if I hadn't started small. You can't jump to the second floor of a house without stairs and you can't fly a Boeing 747 without a progression. You get there by putting one foot in front of the other.

I went from flying a two-seater to flying a four-seater with a larger engine. Next I flew a "tail dragger," then an airplane with a constant speed propeller and an even bigger engine, then a plane with retractable landing gear, etc.

I loved it, and I still love learning new things.

There isn't one right path. There are many.
I believe I could have chosen any profession and prospered.

Our new family.

A pilot even on the water.

ALCOHOL

I remember my stepdad falling on his way to dinner. He had had polio, so he used canes most of the time. After a few drinks he would try to get from the living room to the dining room without his canes, using the wall instead. He could have done it, too, if he hadn't been drunk. But in his stocking feet, on a slippery wooden floor, it was a disaster. Sitting at the dinner table, listening to him fall, we would wait, cringing.

I was the only one he would let help him up. My mother and brothers sat at the table, waiting. Dad and I would make it to the dining room and sit down without a word. We didn't talk about it. *This was our normal.*

One night, Dad did a face plant into his mashed potatoes. He came up grinning—white goo all over his face. I couldn't take any more. I stood up and screeched my chair under the table.

"Where do you think you're going?" my mother asked.

"To my room. I don't have to eat dinner with a drunk."

"Show some respect. Your father isn't drunk, he's just tired after a long day at work."

Seriously? I left the room, shaking my head in frustration.

Mom told us never to talk about Dad's drinking to anyone. *Especially his boss.* This wasn't uncommon in the sixties and seventies. People were private. We knew that if Dad lost his job, Mom would have to support the family by herself. So we kept up the facade. *Yes, there's an elephant in our living room. Just walk around it.*

Dad never got abusive or mean. He tickled and wrestled too hard, but eventually he would stop. We said it was because his arms were so strong from using canes; he didn't know his own strength. Still, he never hit us. He was a quiet drunk who would stay up late reading or watching movies. We loved him and always made excuses for him:

"He gets drunk after one drink because he has no body-mass below his waist due to the polio."

"He's still sad because his first wife left him and took his little boy."

"He has had a hard day."

"His boss is giving him trouble."

No, he just drank to drink. He was an alcoholic.

When I was in high school, Dad fell on the ice in Budapest and hurt his back. Now we had a new excuse for the drinking: he drank because he was in pain. On days when Dad was hung over and Mom had already left for work, his boss would call looking for him. I was supposed to say that Dad was sick, or that he was already gone, or make some other lame excuse for his not being at work. When I would protest, Dad ordered me to answer the phone. Some days his boss yelled at me for lying. It was a no-win situation.

The summer I graduated high school, I was on my way to visit my grandparents in Indiana. I happened to sit next to my doctor from my bout with mononucleosis that year, on the same plane, on his way to a medical conference. He mentioned that he'd removed a cyst from my dad's ear a few weeks before, and that Dad's breath smelled like liquor. I didn't know what to say.

We started talking about the situation at my house. We brainstormed about getting our two families together for a picnic, so he and Dad could talk. That never happened. This doctor, a man I liked and respected, told me that Dad would lose his job if I did not get him to stop drinking.

Me? What could I do? I had already tried everything… I would storm into the house with a bottle of booze I'd found hidden in Dad's workshop or car and confront him… I'd get angry with him for making Mom cry the night before and he would agree to slow down the drinking. My brother would pour Dad's scotch down the sink and then dilute what was left with colored water.

I wanted to get as far away from home as possible. Part of me felt that the drinking was my fault. I'd overheard my dad telling my mom that he hated teenage girls. Of course I took this to heart and blamed myself. *Hadn't I always been a brat?* I *was* a tough child to have around the house, angry and combative. I chose Colorado State for college, almost two thousand miles from Florida.

When I came home for my eighteenth birthday, I received a birthday spanking I will never forget. It hurt so badly that I was in tears by the third swat. No one could get Dad to stop. He was drunk, and didn't realize how badly he was hurting me. I didn't care if I never came home again. I was tired of making excuses for him, and tired of my mom defending him. I didn't care if he died.

He did. He died later that year. I cared more than I ever imagined. I loved him.

What doesn't kill you really does make you stronger.

We loved to fish, and we often went to the Florida Keys.

Us kids with Gabby.

DRUGS

Gainesville, Florida is famous for the University of Florida Gators and Gatorade, but when I was growing up, it was also famous for Gainesville Green. Gainesville Green was a potent type of marihuana that grew everywhere, including on the land behind our house. I'm sure my parents didn't know it was there, but we kids did.

There was a time when my career aspirations included being an FBI agent. I knew you couldn't do drugs and be with the FBI, so I was a straight-laced, goody-two shoes girl. Almost everyone in my grade smoked pot—it wasn't cool not to. One day, in biology class, we were out hunting for specimens in the woods. I was collecting with a group of pot smokers, and they passed their joint to me. To be cool, I took a toke. After all, who would know? Certainly not the FBI... Well, that one hit was strong. I went back to class stoned.

Mrs. Allen, my biology teacher, was awesome. Her husband was Ross Allen, the renowned reptile expert. Marlin Perkins (the television host of Mutual of Omaha's *Wild Kingdom*) and Lloyd Bridges *(Sea Hunt)* often came to her house for dinner, and we loved to hear stories about them. I babysat for her grandson. The look of disappointment on Mrs. Allen's face when she realized I was stoned kept me from ever smoking during school again.

I'm not going to lie and say I never tried pot again. There was a party I was invited to, where everyone was getting high. I had put $5 into a collection at school that day, for pot-laced brownies. How could we tell which ones they were? They were in a shoebox with powdered sugar on top. When they came, I chowed down a few and felt... nothing. So I ate two more. Nothing...

There I was, stone cold sober, sitting in a room with some kids who were getting high on LSD. It was one of the scariest nights of my life. One guy was moaning and rolling around on the bed, screaming. When his trip got worse, everyone else left because he was too loud. I stayed. I was afraid for him, and tried to talk him out of whatever demons he was seeing. Finally, he came down from his "trip." I decided to go home. On my way out, the person with the "real" brownies was walking in. I snagged one to eat on the drive home. A few bites later, I was reeling. I walked into my parent's bridge club and pretended to be straight. "Why are you home so early? Wasn't the party fun?" they asked. I was sure they could tell I was stoned, but I answered their questions and went to lie down on my spinning bed.

Suffice it to say, the tripping experience scared me out of trying any LSD *ever*. But pot seemed innocuous—a good relaxant. One day five of us were sitting under the alcove at the library at school, talking and smoking. A policeman came up the walkway and we panicked, jamming the joint under the floor mat. "Just checking the door, kids. Just checking the door." *Talk about relief.* I saw all my aspirations of being in the FBI go up in smoke. I decided it just wasn't worth the chance of getting caught.

At college, I rarely smoked dope. It was too expensive, and my friends had better things to do. But years later, when I was teaching flying in Oregon, everyone smoked and it was a normal part of relaxing on the weekends. One morning I was flying with a student after smoking the night before. My reflexes weren't fast enough to stop him from landing the airplane too hard for my tastes. I realized my reaction times were affected, even twelve hours after smoking. It wasn't worth the risk, and I loved flying enough to make the decision not to smoke anymore.

It was one of the hardest things I've ever done because I loved the relaxing feeling only pot could give me. I still went to parties and watched my friends smoking, without judgment. But I refrained. And I noticed something. The friends who got stoned every day or even every weekend, slowly dropped their career aspirations. They took routine jobs and left their dreams behind.

Pot may not be addictive, but for some people, I think it relaxes them too much. They don't care passionately about anything anymore. That's a problem for me. I need passion and I have big goals and dreams.

Some chances just aren't worth taking.

Age twenty with my Cessna 140

Our Friday Afternoon Club on Horsetooth Reservoir. When John Denver sang "Rocky Mountain High" on the radio, we would stand up and put our hands over our hearts!

San Francisco Bay

COLLEGE

It takes a long time to build flight time when you can only afford an hour lesson every two weeks. By the end of high school, I had 21.1 hours in my logbook. I had soloed and taken a cross-country flight. Bob, one of the instructors, let me fly the helicopter to the fair and back every day for a week while selling tickets for the flight school. The reason I had so few hours was that I came down with mononucleosis and lost my job at the airport.

My real dad's death was service-connected, so we received support payments each month from the government after he died. My mother saved every penny of his veteran's benefits for my brother's and my college, and I'm still grateful beyond words. Mom wouldn't let me use the money for flying lessons, only for college. I decided to major in Environmental Health to help save the world from pollution and disease.

My mother wasn't thrilled by this career choice either. She thought I should concentrate on my "strengths," which were writing, languages, and the arts. My classes were mostly science and math. Consequently, college was hard. I had no chemistry background, by my own choice. But I loved microbiology and the classes in my major, and, of course, my math classes were fun. Even though I wasn't going to be a doctor or veterinarian, many of my classes were pre-requisites for those careers, so the competition was fierce. I took statistics, biological calculus, three years of chemistry, anatomy, biology, civil engineering, and three years of microbiology. I studied hard, but I still had lots of Bs and Cs.

I ran short on money and took a job at McDonald's. I loved it! They had a great training program, and the people I worked with were fun.

Taking my internship in Denver the summer of my junior year, I watched the airplanes taking off and landing at the Fort Collins/ Loveland Airport as I drove by on the freeway. I missed flying. I couldn't see myself inside a laboratory my whole life, analyzing air and water samples. I needed windows.

Nor could I see myself studying communicable diseases. Melanie, the best student in our microbiology classes, contracted tuberculosis while doing a special project for the teacher. Melanie's techniques were impeccable—flawless compared to mine—yet obviously they had not protected her. I shuddered at the thought of working at the Center for Disease Control and injecting myself with AIDS or Ebola.

I loved flying. Why had I stopped? Could I do it for a living? My eyes were 20/30 and the airlines wanted 20/20. But one of my first flight instructors was a female and she wore glasses. I *could* be a flight instructor or corporate pilot… I didn't have to be an airline pilot.

I started taking lessons again. Flying was still fun. This time I was more serious and less apt to count swimming pools. "Working" toward my licenses was so enjoyable that it never seemed like work. I think that is the way it is if you do what you love. I bought a little plane for $3,000, and started building flight time.

***Do what you love.
No one knows you better than you know yourself.***

BUILDING THE COFFIN

In any aviation accident there are always a number of mistakes made, not just one. Old, salty pilots call this phenomenon *building the coffin*. A coffin has six sides… count them:

Coffin side number One: I'm flying across the country in my Cessna 140, from Colorado to Florida, after graduating college. I have over one hundred flight hours and I'm a little cocky. This common, low-time pilot tendency to overestimate your abilities is a killer.

Coffin side number Two: I fueled up in Kansas, but neglected to climb a ladder to visually check my gas tanks. I had old gauges with cork floats that are inaccurate, so this was a major mistake on my part. The line boy hadn't "topped them off" like I had asked. So I took off with less fuel than I thought I had.

Coffin side number Three: The clouds are scattered. I pulled back on the yoke, climbed above them, and headed east. As the clouds become more broken and solid, instead of turning around, I was busy looking at my map, finding radio frequencies now that I couldn't see the ground. Doing a 180-degree turn is what I was taught to do in this situation. Foolishly I flew on. Shoulda, woulda, coulda…

Coffin side number Four: I didn't realize the winds aloft were so strong. Apparently I didn't pay enough attention during my weather briefing. I can't get my navigational radios to tune. I can't figure out what's wrong. (I later learn that I'm drifting south so fast that I am out of range of all stations I try. Thinking I'm further north, I'm picking the wrong ground stations and none of them work.)

Coffin side number Five: I'm on top of a solid overcast, unsure of my position—lost. My heart was racing. Now it *is* too late to turn back. I've got to get underneath the overcast and figure out where I am. My fuel gauges are bouncing off empty. *Are they really empty?* I don't have a clue because I never checked my tanks so that I could time my fuel usage.

I know the statistics. A pilot who hasn't been trained to fly using instruments has less than a minute before they develop vertigo and become disoriented inside the clouds without a horizon for reference. Still, I start a spiral turn through a small hole, going in and out of the clouds. I have no choice—there is no other way down. I quickly become confused and disoriented, so I level out. Catching my breath, I try again, praying, keeping my turn steeper so that I stay mostly clear of the clouds.

This time my turn worked. I'm safely below the clouds. Eureka! I start looking for an airport or any familiar reference on my sectional map. Nothing matches. Unbeknownst to me, I'm over Arkansas instead of Missouri. I decide to look for an airport before my engine runs out of gas.

When I can't find an airport, I start looking for fields. I'm scared, but I can do this. I've practiced engine failures lots of times. I line up on a suitable pasture. Just before touchdown, I see the horses. I add power and climb, searching until I find another flat, grassy field. Most of the fields have power lines or obstacles. Finally, I find one I like.

I fly a modified pattern, with a steep descent, and land in the grass. *I should have taken a college class in agriculture.* The "grass" is tall alfalfa. It wraps around my wheels, almost causing me to ground loop. (A ground loop in a tail dragger is easy to do, and the saying is there are those that have and those that will. It is when the wing tip touches, whipping the plane to a stop.) I put both feet on the left brake and rudder pedal, trying desperately to keep the plane straight... but my right wing tip still sinks toward the ground. Miraculously, the wing levels as I come to a stop. Breathing fast I open my door and step out. I stand there, getting my bearings—shaking.

A FARMER AND his hired man drove up in a pickup. They were congenial and didn't seem to mind at all that I'd ripped up their field. We checked the plane for damage, but there was none. They offered to call a local crop duster to bring some gas.

The farmer and his wife fed me grilled cheese sandwiches and Arkansas pickles. They introduced me to everyone in Clarksville, Arkansas. They showed me around their farm and their barn full of hundreds of turkeys. *Now I'm worried anew. The one thing you don't want to do, I've been told, is fly low over a turkey farm because they panic, and run into a corner and suffocate.* The farmer told me not to worry—turkeys are so dumb they lose some to suffocation every day.

While I was eating lunch, the hired man mowed a runway, saying they were going to cut the alfalfa next week anyway. The crop duster brought a few gallons of gas, and offered to fly my plane down to his strip. I didn't know where his airport was, nor did I have much experience flying out of short fields, so I just thanked him and said yes. Watching him take off, he almost hit the treetops and I wondered if I'd made the right decision.

The farmer's wife gave me two bottles of Arkansas pickles as a souvenir of my visit and drove me to the duster's strip. Her husband was blind, so he couldn't drive! The duster topped off the plane, and this time I climbed up and checked the fuel level. He says the takeoff was exciting for him, too. I paid the crop-duster for gas and taxied out for takeoff.

Pushing the power in, the wheels stuck in the mud. The plane rotated so that I was looking out the front windshield at the ground!

Quickly I pulled the power off and the tail settled back down. Slowly I pushed the power back in, accelerating gradually over the soft ground. I took off for Little Rock, Arkansas. *What a day.*

***Coffin side number Six*:** The lid: Thank goodness I didn't make one more mistake to close the coffin. I can't tell you how much safer I am as a pilot after this incident. The cockiness is gone, replaced by a sense of elation. I'm alive!

Staying alive is a good thing.

I made it from Colorado to Florida in my Cessna 140!

OLD TIME ROCK 'N' ROLL

I spent all my money on my pilot licenses after college. I sold my airplane to continue my training, waitressed, pumped gas, and did anything else I could to earn money. Living in Orlando, Florida, married to a flight instructor, we were both working for a man with an idea for a new form of sky writing, called "sky typing." I was at the airport getting parts, thinking about the free concert I listened to the night before. Fleetwood Mac was in town, and their music had drifted across the lake through my open bedroom window. Their plane was sitting on the ramp as I walked toward the hangar, and their pilot saw me ogling it and offered me a tour. When I stopped at the cockpit instead of heading straight for the "living room," he asked me if I flew. He said they were looking for pilots who had their mechanic license, and my husband did. He was interviewed and hired immediately as a copilot on their four-engine Vickers Viscounts.

Goodbye Orlando. Hello California! I was hired as a flight attendant for "Go, Inc." after an interview to determine that I was not a "groupie" and could handle the job. Rock groups can be big babies, and take "special handling." Go Inc. painted the airplane tails before each tour with each group's logo so people would think the rock groups owned the plane. My uniform was lace-up blue jeans and a tight shirt with no bra. The airplanes were decked out with curtains, comfy sofas, lounge chairs, and televisions. The idea was to help the bands relax and feel "at home" because many of them were afraid of flying. The stereo system, with twelve speakers, was "killer" because the groups liked to listen to music—usually their own! Video games were just invented, and we had the first one: Pong.

Shopping before each flight was my favorite activity. The band manager handed our captain thousands of dollars at the beginning of each tour. They gave me the shopping list—expensive cheeses, meats, snacks, and booze. The limousine took me to the grocery store and waited outside while I shopped. After being on a tight budget for years, always scrimping and buying cheaper brands, it was fun to go wild. Then the bag boys pushed the carts out to the waiting limo, while I headed to the liquor store to buy Tanqueray gin, Johnny Walker Red and Black, Mateus and Blue Nun wine, Heineken beer—twice what the groceries cost. Onlookers probably thought I was important getting into my limo with thirty bags of groceries and hundreds of dollars-worth of booze. It was fun to pretend to be famous!

Getting ready to move to California
to go on tour with America in 1977.

Thirty-five years later with Dewey and Geri of America.

Once, at a grocery store in the Midwest, the cashier was furious with me. The bill came to $340, a huge amount in 1977. Pepperidge Farm cookies were a necessity, as were Rondelé Cheese and Planter's Sesame Cashew Nut Mix. I had twenty bags of Tootsie Roll Pops because the lead singer of America only liked red ones and I had to sort them out. The rest of the groceries were mainly chips, cookies, and candy. Angrily, the cashier demanded, "How can you feed this crap to your children? What kind of mother are you?"

She thought I was a mother? Just for fun, I went along with the charade. Straight faced, I replied, "But they like it. I just want them to be happy."

"You should be ashamed. This stuff will rot their teeth and make them sick." She fumed and fussed at me the entire time she was bagging my groceries. To this day the lady probably tells her friends how much junk food I bought for my children. She wasn't too far from the truth. Lots of rock stars *act* like spoiled children.

I flew numerous bands around that summer. One day I threw away a pizza laden with cocaine. The guys were so stoned that someone had spilled a whole Baggie of white powder into the grease. Sometimes the air on the airplane was so thick with the smell of marijuana that it almost made me sick. My ex-husband liked to tease the captain. "Hey, Roy, don't those red lights looks pretty? Do you feel kind of funny?" We had orders to pull the stairs up if anyone looking like law enforcement was on the airport ramp. There were too many drugs onboard to take a chance. Once, I found one of the band members riding the hotel elevator up and down, lost and stoned; trying to remember what city he was in. I helped him to his floor, but not to his room. (I'm not *that* friendly.)

I had to buy all the magazines the groups wanted, too, including *Playboy*, *Hustler*, *Penthouse*, *Chic*, and *Forum*. The clerks probably thought I was a pervert. One of the pornographic magazines contained a new gimmick—the first scratch and sniff issue. Everyone in the band took turns looking at it, passing it around, scratching and sniffing. Dave Dickey, one of the band members in America, asked, "Who buys these *disgusting rags*?" Red faced, I admitted that I did. They were on the list. "Who put them on the list?" he asked the rest of the guys. No one would admit to having requested them, but everyone read them!

Flights were usually short—less than three hours. The Vickers Viscounts were luxurious but slow. Conveniently, the concerts took place in cities located close together. Takeoff time was late morning, so I served lunch. My sandwiches were like those in Lawrence Sander's novels with Harry Bosch—loaded with meats, cheeses, vegetables, and condiments. I made them to order in the galley, after serving drinks. The guys would play poker the entire flight, eating and drinking, laughing and talking. Willy, America's drummer, claimed he made $5000 a flight winning at poker.

Dewey and Scott.

Playing poker: Willy (center) made easy money.

When the bands wanted a change of pace, they asked for fast foods like pizza, fried chicken, tacos, or hamburgers. Drive-through employees were always shocked to see a limousine pull in and order twelve buckets of chicken or thirty pizzas. As usual, they craned their necks to see who was inside. I'm sure they were disappointed to see just me.

Concerts were amazing. We had backstage passes and, unless we were flying out right after the concert, we always went. Trashcans of pricey beers and wine filled the backstage area, along with tables of food for the hordes of people who were always milling around—guests of the band, groupies, and friends. There was a trailer outside for those who wanted drugs. It was easy, I think, for the groups to blow millions of dollars with so many "friends."

The bands brought guests on the plane with them—members of their backup bands, girlfriends, wives, and even groupies. One day one of the guys came on with a groupie in tow. The girl had her thumb in her mouth and a teddy bear under one arm. She wanted "gwape juice." I gave them their drinks, and then he led her to the back of the Viscount and locked the door. The turbulence that day came from inside the airplane, and the band laughed as noises emanated from the rear. We had to roust them after landing! She trailed off after him, thumb back in place.

The flight cables in the Vickers Viscount ran through the ceiling. One of the groups figured this out—don't ask me how. They would jam their fists or other objects into the padded ceiling, trying to locate one of the cables. If they found an elevator cable, the plane would climb or descend. An aileron cable produced a left or right turn. They were too stoned to care, but we did. The company had a list of bands we refused to fly.

Backstage at concerts was always fun!

We had six Vickers Viscounts and flew rock groups:
The Eagles, Fleetwood Mac, Crosby Stills and Nash, America, and others.

My salary was $800 per month, plus $800 for expenses. The tips at the end of the tours made up for the low pay. One flight attendant received over $3000 in tips for her summer tour, but most of us received smaller amounts. It added up, and was enough to pay for my multi-engine rating at the end of the summer. We also got to keep the extra food and drink after the tours.

Some groups were known for their obscenity and violence. Once in a while a group member or the entire band would rape flight attendants. These attacks never went public. The performers paid dearly for their "fun" and the girl left quietly, with less money than she deserved.

I was scheduled to be the flight attendant for *Bad Company.* Management decided I couldn't handle their shenanigans and assigned another flight attendant instead. She was rumored to be an ex-hooker, and they thought she could handle them. I was upset initially, but after hitching a ride on their airplane one night, I decided the decision was a good one. They were crude and raunchy and out of control. One of them grabbed me in the crotch and lifted me two feet into the air. "Just checking to see how much you weigh, babe. One hundred and twenty, eh?" he asserted in his strong, British accent. I was too shocked and astonished to tell him he was exactly right.

We flew the Commodores on the one airplane we had with fifty seats, because they wanted to bring their roadies and stage-hands with them. They were a nice group of guys, even nicer after I was serving lunch and couldn't remember who had ordered a sand-wich. At first they chided me for thinking they all looked alike, and made me stand on the armrests and yell out, "Who had the chicken sandwich with sprouts and avocado?" When the only white guy on the plane claimed it, I was in like Flynn. Their manager, Al, took me under his wing, getting me a seat next to him in the third row at concerts if we weren't backstage. Lionel Ritchie was with the group, and I loved his voice, but I liked Clyde the best. Clyde joked around a lot, especially about their uniforms—air-conditioned $2000 monkey suits, he called them.

At first I envied the lifestyles of the groups we flew. As the summer wore on, I realized that Life in the Fast Lane, is not all that it is cracked up to be. How would you ever know whether someone liked you for you or for your fame and fortune? Too many of the rockers were hanging on to their sanity by a tenuous thread, getting psychiatric help for their issues. The season wound down, and we moved on, but I never forgot the summer of 1977.

I never want to be famous....

My America Stage Pass.

I loved Utah, especially Goblin Valley and Lake Powell.

Our mine site being built.

GOOD C'OAL MANIPULATION

I found a job flying river rafters and their gear in a Cessna 206 in Green River, Utah. I would be picking up rafters after their float. I resigned before I ever got off the ground. The raft frame was made of two by fours, and they tied it to the outside of the aircraft between the tail and the cabin. Landing in any sort of a crosswind, you couldn't straighten the plane out for landing, as it blocked the flow of air over the rudder. The FAA had violated two of the pilots who flew for the rafting company; the other one was dead.

My degree in Environmental Health was a Godsend. The owner of the coal mine, who my ex was flying for, hired me to be the Health and Safety Inspector. I went to certification classes and, when I wasn't inspecting the facility, I helped analyze the coal with my chemistry background. As a perk, I could fly their Cessna 206 to and from the mine site to build hours.

Our boss, Buddy, was a shyster and a manipulator. I liked him at first, but not once I got to know him. Friendly and easy to talk to, he played games with people's heads. He had the local citizens eating out of his hand because he had $14 million of Chase Manhattan Bank's money to spend.

Buddy hired half the county to work for him. I saw him turn husbands against wives and fathers against sons. Brothers turned against brothers, and lifelong friends became enemies. Our boss would wine and dine everyone, then pry information out of them once they were drunk. It was amazing to watch him at work. He had so much information at his disposal that he could exploit anyone. But he didn't stop there.

When the bank representatives came out from New York to check on the operation, our boss wined and dined them, too. Buddy remodeled a hotel and brought in a chef. No expense was spared. He provided the bank reps with hookers and got them drunk, so they were badly hung over the next day.

Utah in the summer is hot and dry, with thermals and unstable air. The coal mine was two and a half hours by car on a winding road, or less than an hour by plane. Either way they chose, the bank representatives were worthless when they arrived at the mine. After a bumpy flight in a small plane, the bankers spent most of their visit puking in the dry, Utah dust. Their reviews of the mine were always exemplary, because they were too sick to know or care.

Our boss spent money like it was water. He bought pristine mobile homes to live and work in, brand new Blazers to drive, and the newest and best mining equipment. He built a huge train-loading facility in Green River. He planned to sell the coal to Nevada Power, so Buddy had us fly him to Vegas every few weeks to meet with them. Our rooms were always complimentary at the Desert Inn, because our boss was a big gambler in more ways than one. We had expansive suites with sunken living rooms, three televisions, marble bathrooms with huge tubs, balconies, and Jacuzzis. Life was good.

Bill, from Kentucky, came out to set up an air jig to clean the coal. There was no water nearby, so the idea was to "float" the coal on air and move the rock out on a separate conveyor belt. Lots of companies still use this technology, but it was new at the time. Unfortunately, the coal was so bad that it was practically rock, so the machine wouldn't work.

"You must be doing it wrong," my boss insisted. "Your machine's junk."

Bill was young and easily intimidated. He shook his head and made adjustments, but couldn't figure out what was wrong.

Bill argued that it could be the coal wasn't good enough quality. Buddy would bring Bill to the lab and ask us what our last sample of coal tested. It was always high—higher than the junk coal from our mines. Buddy never told us where these fantastic samples came from, and he never told Bill. He just smiled and looked at Bill as if to say, "not good enough?"

Coal quality is based on British Thermal Units (BTU), but we assayed it for sulfur, carbon, moisture, and ash as well. Nevada Power paid on BTU values but coal from our mine was rarely over 8500 BTU. They wouldn't accept coal less than 9500, and would dock us if it were that low. Anything above 10,500 BTU paid a bonus. Nevada Power's analysts were behind in their sampling and our coal made it to the boilers before it was tested. Our first and last load of coal to Nevada Power coked up their boilers so badly they had to dynamite them out.

One night our boss got drunk and swore us to secrecy—a secret I am now breaking since he is dead. Buddy admitted that the mine was a fraud—he won the land in a poker game. Then he found a man dying of cancer who needed money badly enough to fake the core samples. *There was no good coal.* The good samples we had been analyzing were from Colorado. Not Utah. Not our coal.

Buddy had taken on a partner from California, and lied to him, too. When the whole house of cards was ready to fall, Buddy showed up with a shotgun, pretending the coal mine was a good operation his partner was trying to swindle him out of. The partner acted predictably and bought our boss out. The mine was bankrupt within six months.

The tips from flying the rock groups had allowed me to get a multi-engine rating. I had a few hundred hours flying the Cessna 206 to and from the mine site, and the new owner sent my ex-husband and me to Texas for training on a Learjet 23. I would be a copilot on a Lear! My exhilaration didn't last. The Lear was too expensive to fly to and from a coalmine with no coal. Three trips to Green River, landing on a short runway with no reversers, meant a brake change that cost $1200. Besides, the Lear was a gas-guzzler. My new boss leased it to a company that operated charters, and I was out of work, again.

I still hadn't found anyone I aspired to be, but I met lots of people I didn't want to be like. Power and money were becoming four letter words to me. When the mine went under I decided to teach flying. I now had seventy hours of Learjet time, with only six hundred total hours. I was thinking seriously about an airline job now, and I needed more flight time.

I take it back. Being rich isn't everything either.

Our Lear 23 (no reversers!) in Green River, Utah.

SURVIVAL OF THE FITTEST

Being a flight instructor was my first real job in aviation. It is also the one I enjoyed the most. My ex-husband was hired at Georgia Pacific in Portland, Oregon as a pilot and mechanic. I applied at nearby flight schools.

The Beechcraft school at the Portland International Airport was reluctant to hire me because I had so little time in their planes. I had flown Cessnas, Pipers, and Mooneys but I had minimal time in Beechcrafts. I remember going flying with their chief flight instructor so that he could see what my skills were. My first landing was firm: Beechcrafts landed differently than the Cessnas I was used to. Because I was a new instructor, he didn't want to take a chance.

I went to Troutdale Airport, just east of Portland, to interview. Western Skyways was the Cessna dealer on the field, and I knew how to fly Cessnas. The chief flight instructor, Walt Luelling, took me up in a Cessna 152 to perform takeoffs and landings, stalls, spins, and advanced maneuvers like chandelles. When I taxied in afterwards he said, "You're hired."

I was shocked. It couldn't be that easy. I think I looked at him and said something like, "That's it? You're sure?" He laughed and said yes. Walt didn't play games. He was straightforward and fair. I worked for him for two years and loved my job. The Veteran's Bill was winding down and lots of veterans were flying, using up their money from their service. I had a full schedule and no problem building hours. I often worked seven days a week.

Troutdale is on the west end of the Columbia River Gorge—a giant wind tunnel. Flight instructing doesn't pay well. There are many days that are too windy, too foggy, or too rainy to fly. You have to be flexible, working overtime whenever the weather is good. I caught flak from other instructors for not taking my students up when it was too windy or bumpy, but there was no reason to waste my students' money by having them fly the airplane in conditions that could frighten them or were beyond their capabilities.

Most of the guys instructing viewed teaching as a necessary evil—a way to build flight time so they could get an airline job. They thought I was too cautious and, well, a bit of a girl. But instead of viewing it as a means to an end, I looked forward to each day at the airport. Teaching someone who has a passion to learn is so much fun. People who learn how to fly are often fulfilling a life-long dream or desire. They come to you as eager students, more than willing to try hard and prepare for the next lesson. They've saved their hard earned money, often for years, before committing to lessons.

Tracy was one of my favorite students. She was on her last flight with me before taking her private pilot check ride the next day—a certificate that would allow her to take passengers with her in an airplane. While practicing her steep turns, the engine lost power. The plane began to shudder and shake. Frightened, she shrieked, "You've got it." I started to take control, and then realized she would be on her own, possibly with passengers, in a day's time.

"No, you've got it. What are you going to do?" I asked her calmly, even though I had never lost an engine before, either.

"I don't know. Land? You take it!"

Tracy was stubborn, but so am I. "Yes, land, but where? We've practiced this lots of times," I prodded.

"Estacada? It's the closest and we're high enough."

Her knowledge began to kick in, and her confidence returned. She did a beautiful approach and landing. She was a little high and a little fast, but she landed the plane by herself and she did it safely. Her confidence soared. The examiner was impressed by her flying the next day, and also noted that she seemed to believe in herself and her abilities. She earned her private pilot license with flying colors.

Letting people make mistakes instead of correcting them too soon is crucial in flight training. They learn better when they discover their own errors. I found that I learned right along with them. Dana, another female student, had long fingernails, high heels, and short skirts. The male employees at Skyways loved to watch her preflight, especially when she climbed up onto the step to check the top surface of the wings and the fuel. I had my work cut out for me. I got her to wear appropriate shoes and worry more about getting the carburetor heat in quickly than breaking a nail. Soon she was a pro... a knowledgeable and capable pilot.

One student was passed from instructor to instructor, and I was his last chance before our flight school kicked him out. He didn't seem too bad doing turns and basic air work, and I started to relax. Then we were on final approach. He got lower and lower; slower and slower. I took the plane away from him when I realized he wasn't going to make any corrections. He started laughing. *What a psycho.* Turns out he got his kicks by scaring instructors. We kicked him out.

Another one of my students was from Vietnam. He claimed to have "left" his logbook behind, with hundreds of hours of flight time. Indeed, he flew very well and I had no reason to doubt his story after flying with him for fifteen hours. I was ready to solo him.

We were on final approach with landing flaps. I was giving him no help, pretending I wasn't there, in anticipation of letting him go up by himself. He needed to add power, because we were getting a little low and slow. All of a sudden, the plane dropped like a rock.

"Kath! Kath, are you all right?" Jim, the Troutdale tower controller, squawked through the radio.

I couldn't answer him. I was too busy trying to stay alive. I felt like an octopus, pushing in carburetor heat, lowering the nose, adding full power—just trying to keep the plane in the air. We almost hit the trees.

"I am now," I answered Jim at last. I could hardly believe how close I had come to crashing. My heart was racing and my breath was coming in short gasps. Assessing the situation, I realized he had put all the flaps up at once.

"Why did you do that?" I asked my student as soon as I landed and we were taxiing in.

"Too much drag, getting too slow," he explained, all color drained from his face.

"Flaps are drag, but they're also lift. You needed to add power." I didn't yell at him, but he could see how scared I was. I now knew he had lied to me about his flight time. I believe he had flown before, but only in the backseat of a transport plane as an observer. Maybe he felt he had "lost face," an Asian expression for embarrassing oneself badly. I never saw him again. Thank goodness I hadn't soloed him—he would have killed himself.

Jim Shotwell was one of my best students and I loved flying with him. I had signed him off for his private pilot license the year before, and he passed with flying colors. The FAA examiner couldn't sing Jim's praises loudly enough after the check ride. He did an awesome job.

Jim loved flying. He was always trying to improve his skills. Now he was working on his instrument rating. It was a clear day and Jim was under the "hood"—a plastic device you strap to your head so that you can see only the instruments but not your surroundings. We were navigating to a VOR just north of Portland, Oregon. *(VOR stands for Very High Frequency Omni Directional Range and pilots can fly from VOR to VOR in the clouds, without looking at the ground.)*

I knew Jim hated being off course even slightly. As we flew closer to the station, the margin for error becomes less and the needle gets very sensitive. There was also wind at our altitude that he was not correcting his heading for. Whenever Jim got slightly off course, he kept adjusting the knob on the instrument instead of turning, or "crabbing," the airplane into the wind. I had seen him do this before, but not as persistently. Before I always corrected him. Today I decided to let him do it his way.

Looking out my window at the station shaped like a big, white, bowling pin, I tried not to laugh. *Jim was making perfect circular turns around the VOR station.* He would never cross over the VOR with this technique.

Finally, after three or four perfect turns he looked up at me, perplexed and perspiring. He exclaimed in frustration, "I can't find the station." I pointed to the station almost directly beneath us and cracked up laughing. Jim started laughing too. Today, thirty-five years later, he is still a safe, proficient pilot who now owns an AT-6.

One of my female students was working on her flight instructor rating. Part of the course included spins, a maneuver Tara said she would never do. I told her she couldn't get her license without knowing how to do them. We tussled, and she decided to change instructors. But no one else would sign her off without performing spins either. She went home to eastern Oregon.

A week later she returned. If I would just lie and sign her off, she said, she would be fine. Her reasoning was she would never let a student get into a spin in the first place.

"What if they get into a spin while out practicing stalls and can't recover? What if a student you train dies because you never taught them spin recovery?" I asked.

Finally, she gritted her teeth and agreed to learn spin recovery. We climbed to 8000 feet in the practice area, an altitude that made her feel safer. We started with easy stalls, a maneuver she was also afraid of. I showed her that if the little ball on the turn indicator were off center at all, the plane would "drop off" sharply in the other direction. She said she would never let it get off center.

I told her she couldn't hover over or control her students that tightly—they had to make their own mistakes and learn. Finally, she acquiesced and let me show her how safely the plane could even recover on its own once you let go of the controls. She got over her fear of stalls, and we started on spins. Soon she could recover perfectly, safely, and with little altitude loss. She would never like spins, but at least she wasn't afraid. When the FAA examiner signed her off as a Certified Flight Instructor, I knew she would be a great teacher.

As I said before, teaching doesn't pay well. When the weather is bad and you can't fly, you don't get paid. People get sick and cancel, leaving a huge hole in your schedule. I earned a whopping ten thousand dollars a year teaching. But the hours I logged and the experience I gained made it worth it.

Skyways bid on a bank courier contract, to pick up cancelled checks from all over Oregon and fly them to Portland. A meeting was held, and the boss of the jet department, Dave, told all the instructors we would be expected to fly one day a week on "check runs" in a Cessna 182. The contract only allowed for a certain number of days with a twin-engine plane, since a twin-engine was so much more expensive to operate. There are many days when the icing is bad over Cascade Mountains… that's why Boeing does their icing tests there. I asked who would decide when the weather was bad enough to use the twin, since the 182 was not equipped with de-icing boots on the wings. Dave said management would determine whether it was bad enough to put a twin on the route.

I didn't want to give someone else control over the safety of my flight, and I had seen too many of my friends die. I refused to fly the check runs. Dave told me it was non-negotiable—all instructors would fly the checks. He asked me if I really thought he would make a decision that could kill me. I told him I wouldn't be much of a pilot if I let him make life-threatening decisions that should be up to me. I had a full schedule of students who would be glad to follow me down the street to Blue Skies, the other flight school on the field. Dave talked to Walt and decided to let me opt out.

Steve Keyes, another instructor and good friend, had the same reservations I did. I begged him to turn them down, because he had a lot of students, too. Steve said his schedule was not as full as mine—he needed the money and he had a wife to support. Besides, the other flight instructors were doing it and they thought I was a wuss. So, Steve agreed to fly checks and I didn't.

While I was instructing at Troutdale, there were many days I couldn't fly because of bad weather. Troutdale is at the west end of the Columbia Gorge, so high winds, fog, and icing conditions are all too common. On days I couldn't work, I would drive to the Hillsboro

FAA office west of Portland and take written tests. One winter the weather was so bad that I took the Ground Instructor, Instrument Ground Instructor, and Airline Transport Pilot (ATP) tests. On a lark, I decided to drive over and take the Dispatcher written, too, because it was almost identical to the ATP test. The secretary laughed when I walked in the door because I was back again.

The Dispatcher written was an easy test, especially after the weekend ground school I had attended to prepare for the ATP. I was almost finished when one of the examiners walked into the room and leaned over my shoulder to see what test I was taking. "You're not qualified to take this test," Don announced. Asserting myself, I told him I met all the requirements. He disagreed, and asked why I wanted to take it. I told him it might be useful to have if an airline hired me. Don reached out, picked up my test and tore it to shreds. I protested, angrily, to no avail. Disgusted, I walked out.

"Done already?" the secretary asked.

"Only because Don tore up my test," I told her.

She couldn't believe it.

What gave him the right? All the way home I vented to my car, a little Datsun B210 that always listened. I received a call from the head boss of the Hillsboro FAA office at home that night. He asked me what I was doing the next day. "Nothing," I told him. It was my day off. "Can you come back over and finish taking the Dispatcher written?"

"I can, but I didn't think tomorrow was a day you were open for written exams," I answered, confusion in my voice.

"We're open for you," he announced.

I showed up the next morning, said hello to my friend the secretary, and she escorted me into the testing area. "Don had to tape your entire test back together," she laughed. "Just copy the answers onto the new test, and complete it."

It didn't take me long to finish. I stood up to leave, but was intercepted by Don's boss. He brought me into his office and asked me how I did. I told him I aced it. Then he apologized profusely for Don's behavior and asked if I would accept Don's apology, even though his actions were inexcusable. I agreed, and Don was called in. I could tell he didn't want to apologize, but had been told to. His boss seemed to think he was lucky I hadn't filed a complaint. I left, unsure whether I should be angry or happy.

A month later I ran into Don in the crowded lobby at Western Skyways. He asked me, rather snidely, how I had done. "A 95% on the ATP and a 98% on the Dispatcher," I answered.

He followed me out the door to the pop machine, where no one else was around. "No airline will ever hire you," he said. "I should have torn up your ATP, too."

Shaking my head in disgust, I walked out to give a flight lesson. As a pilot, I didn't realize I had any power over the FAA, and I was a little afraid of them. Now I wish I had called his boss back and filed a complaint. (He was fired the next year, when he harassed someone else, so in the end, it didn't matter.) If I had a dollar for every time someone in power tried to stop me from achieving my goals as a pilot, I would be a wealthy woman today. Some men have egos the opposite size of their... oh never mind.

One of my students needed to be dropped off in Twin Falls, Idaho. The weather took a turn for the worse, so I got stuck in Boise because, of course, I wouldn't fly over the mountains with icing in the clouds in a single engine airplane. I had plenty of time to wander around the airport. The Forest Service had beautiful turboprops they used for infrared mapping over forest fires. I went into their office and asked what it took to get hired. They gave me an eleven-page application form and had me talk to the Chief Pilot of the Northwest Region. He told me to keep in touch and that they would be hiring for the summer fire season. I filled out the application—a process that took days because it was so involved, and I called every week to let them know I was still interested. I was hired for the 1980 fire season and my days of flight instructing were over.

YEARS LATER, WHEN I returned to Oregon, I ran into the FAA examiner at a wedding. He filled me in on what all the guys from Western Skyways were doing. I asked about Steve. His face fell. "You didn't hear? Steve was scud running in a Cessna 182 because there was icing in the clouds above. He ran into a wall of cumulo-granite and was killed instantly."*

To this day I get a sick feeling in the pit of my stomach when I think about Steve. Even men have trouble standing up for themselves in aviation. I'm glad I didn't have to pretend to be macho to be one of the guys.

Stand up for yourself to stay alive.

*Scud running is flying at low altitudes to avoid clouds.
"Cumulo granite" is pilot talk for mountains inside of clouds.

*Aspen, Colorado. Mountain flying was an important skill to learn,
and my flight school offered a great course in it.*

*Troutdale Airport in Oregon is near the Cascades,
where Boeing does their flight tests for icing.*

Our infrared crew flew a King Air 90, a Merlin, and a Queen Air.

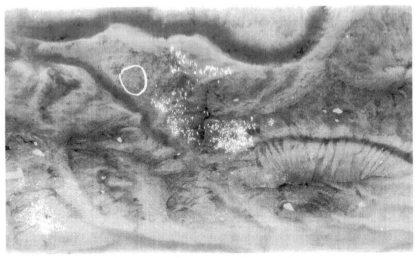

Jerry's infrared imagery was sharp and clear.

INFRARED

Six of us sit in a trailer, reading to stay awake, at the Boise International Airport. Our feet are propped up on our desks and we're all dressed in green uniforms. We could have been leprechauns, but in reality we're infrared pilots for the United States Forest Service. We are on call and bored, waiting for our red phone—what we call the *Bat Phone*—in the center of the room, to ring. California was on fire... there were forest fires everywhere and they still hadn't called us. Like Bruce Wayne and his faithful sidekick, aka Batman and Robin, waiting in their mansion—we sit in our office, waiting to be super heroes.

Before this fire season began, we flew to California to test our equipment. The ground personnel put out smudge pots in the California National Forest. Our infrared equipment can pick up a tiny, six-inch by six-inch fire from 10,000 feet, once everything is calibrated. This year's test flight became one of legend. We picked up a strange series of fires, as well as the pots the ground crews placed for us. Using our imagery, rangers and local sheriffs followed our infrared map on the ground. They arrested an escaped prisoner, a murderer, who thought he was safe hiding in the forest. That's how good our equipment is. We know they'll need us in California.

Only two turboprops are equipped for infrared—a Swearingen Merlin and a Beech King Air 90. We have a Queen Air for backup, and to ferry personnel. All the airplanes are painted orange and white. Last month the Merlin was in Kentucky and I was flying the King Air with Chuck in Montana. In between flights, when there are no fires to fight, we sit on call. Waiting. We take turns flying the missions, and this time Eldon and I are at the top of the list.

The red phone rings. We all jump up as if we've been shot. No one can decide who should answer it. Chuck finally leaps across the desk and catches it on the third ring. He nods, answers yes, hangs up the phone, and announces: "California. Eleven fires so far. They want the Merlin."

Eldon calls Flight Service and files our flight plan. I hurry to the parking lot and retrieve my packed suitcase from the car. I can hardly wait to fly in the Merlin. I do my preflight by flashlight on the dark ramp. There are rumors that the government might turn over the infrared section of the Forest Service to an independent contract group in Canada. I hope not. This is one section of the government that is worth its weight in gold.

Just thinking about the lives saved since infrared has been used to fight fires makes me proud to be a part of this division. No longer are smoke jumpers dropped into the heart of a fire by accident. Infrared imagery makes it possible to pinpoint hot spots and map the movement of the fire. Now jumpers are dropped into the safest, most advantageous areas of the forest where they can do the most good. Of course, wind changes still make firefighting a dangerous business, but every edge you can gain to safely fight a fire is worthwhile.

My captain tonight, Eldon Askelson, likes to talk about his smoke jumper days. He has over 450 jumps under his belt. A strange glimmer comes into his eyes when he talks about his experiences. Listening to him moan and groan each morning when he comes to work, there's no doubt as to why he changed careers. His back has had it. He says walking out of the forest after fighting fire, carrying all the gear, did the most damage to his body. I tell him I would never jump out of a perfectly good airplane.

A figure materializes out of the dark in a huge, green, oversized coat. "Jerry!"

Our infrared technician gives me a big bear hug. "Katy, me love. You and Askelson have this mission?"

I nod. Jerry's a kick. Without him, who would keep us awake? Jerry's humor and songs keep us going long after our bodies say we should be sleeping. Infrared missions are routinely flown at night when the ground temperatures are even. During the day the sun warms all sorts of objects, making it difficult for the interpreters to read the imagery. Rocks show up as hot spots, as do roads and any dark, absorbent surfaces. It's hard to tell which spots are fires and which are not. We have to stay on our toes, no matter how tired we are, and fly night missions.

Everything I know about imagery comes from Jerry. Jerry is a pro at his job, and boasts that even Kodak can't believe how he "pushes" their film to develop great pictures in under a minute. He says the secret is keeping the film cold and he stores it on dry ice. Jerry loads his gear into the nose compartment, along with an ice chest full of film and beer. There aren't any stores open at five in the morning when our workday is complete, so we plan ahead. "Everyone needs a cold beer before bed," Jerry claims.

Lately I've taken to hanging out with Jerry and Eldon on Friday nights. We pick up a couple six packs of beer and head for the Boise junkyard. Yes, the junkyard. The guys are into old cars, and the junkyard is the place they find their parts. Usually we stand around inside drinking beer with the owner until someone decides to amble around the yard. We troop outside, hunting for some random part. Discussions about engines and wheels follow, as well as jokes and ribbing. We roam to our hearts' content.

Last week everyone was crushing beer cans by balancing on one foot, then gently tapping their index fingers on both sides of the can simultaneously. I wasn't quick enough to avoid the entire weight of my body crushing my fingers. *Ow.* The laughter that ensued was hearty, but not mean-spirited. I tried again, successfully: flat can, no fingers crunched. I remember the incredible pain learning that trick. To this day, if I perform the "can trick," I do it with extreme caution.

We board the plane. Jerry busies himself in the back. Eldon arrives and we finish our interior preflights and checklists. The engines start easily, and I call the tower for clearance to taxi. Within minutes we lift off and turn south. Jerry's booming voice comes through the interphone with his rendition of "Yellow Rose of Texas" as we climb higher into the night sky.

NOVEMBER 1980: CALIFORNIA IS BURNING UP.

The Merlin has Omega navigation and a Doppler system. We need accurate latitude and longitude positions to fly our grids over the fires. Ideally we fly parallel lines, followed by perpendicular cross sections. We have to fly plus or minus five degrees on our heading for grid accuracy. We can only vary plus or minus fifty feet in altitude. We also have to be plus or minus ten on airspeed, so the nose can't pitch up or down. If we aren't this exact, the grid lines weave and cross, making it impossible for the ground personnel to read and map the fires.

The King Air is solid and stable as a rock, but it only has Doppler radar and we are constantly flying back over a VOR radio station to reset our drifting navigation system. The Merlin is harder to obtain good imagery because it is more pitch sensitive and not as steady, but we love the Omega guidance in it. Of course the old autopilot is not accurate enough, so Eldon and I take turns hand-flying. *All night.*

After the grid is completed, we fly over a designated ground site at two hundred feet and eject the imagery out of a hole in the bottom of the aircraft. There is a lighted "X" positioned on the ground, and we have the film rolled up in a canister like the ones used at bank drive-through windows. If there is an airport near the fire, we land and hand off the imagery, but usually this isn't the case.

Either way, the imagery has to be "fresh." The information needs to be interpreted and used within hours, before anything changes. We take turns to see who can come closest to our targets on imagery drops. That is the high point of our night! Oh, that and watching Eldon and Jerry chew tobacco and spit into a cup on the center console. Then they dare each other to drink it. Yecch.

There is no way to cover all the fires before dawn. We do our best and cover the major ones. Exhausted, we land at six in the morning. We've rented a "wreck" to drive for the week. We cruise to our hotel—a dump on the east side of town. The guys are chewing and spitting, making brown lines down the sides of our old, white Pontiac. I'm in the middle laughing, trying not to get grossed out. We break out the beer and Jerry is right: a beer does make it easier to fall asleep with the sun coming up.

The plastic sheets crackle every time I turn over and the traffic outside keeps waking me up. We prefer dumps because our per diem is so low. Anything over our piddly per diem comes out of our paychecks, but who ever heard of plastic sheets? The maids are cleaning, banging, and vacuuming. Damn. I've got to sleep to be sharp tonight.

WAKE UP TIME, LATE AFTERNOON.

WE HAVE A full night ahead. They are even calling in the King Air and another crew. There are just too many fires for one airplane to handle. We have to fly overtime to cover all the fires as it is, and legally we can't log all the hours we're flying. Houses are burning up underneath us, and we just can't map it all. It's really smoky. We fly as low as we possibly can without distorting the imagery. Visibility is nonexistent and we hope the terrain is well below us.

WE'VE BEEN HERE over two weeks. It's hard to know where all the other traffic is, even with a helicopter at 12,000 feet assuming the role of Air Traffic Control. We fly out of the smoke and almost hit the Baron lead plane. Scary. Someone wasn't where they were sup-posed to be and it *wasn't* us. It's daylight and the fires are so bad that they're running the infrared crews in all but the hottest time of the day. Now there are four crews and two airplanes. Bombers, jump planes, and all sorts of other reconnaissance share the sky. Sometimes the heat from the fires pops us up higher than our allowed fifty feet, and we have to fly the line all over again.

THANKSGIVING DAY.

NO REST FOR the weary. The firefighters traipse through the hangar, exhausted. Huge boxes of food are set up everywhere. There are all kinds of juices and snacks. The pressed turkey sandwiches have little packets of cranberry sauce paired with them. Little pumpkin pies are wrapped up like Twinkies. I didn't know they made pumpkin pies that small. This has to be the strangest, albeit bountiful, Thanksgiving I've ever had.

Walking through the hangar, we pick up food and stuff it in our pockets. We'll eat it later, during the night. Not because we are hungry, but because we get bored. Flying a grid is so routine. Jerry is stuffing food into his green coat with the big pockets: Twinkies, Ding Dongs, Hostess apple and cherry pies, six boxed drinks, sandwiches, and ten pumpkin pies. People are looking askance at him. Some of the ladies give us dirty looks because we are obviously not smoke jumpers. Ignoring them, I ask if he'll share.

"Not a chance, Katy me love. You need a coat like this." Of course I have my own stash, but my pockets are not as big. Jerry eats *all* of his. Thanksgiving comes and goes. At least we had our feast—a regular junk food delight. As we get a handle on the fires and the season winds down, we take the Merlin to Oregon for much needed maintenance. I get a call from Northwest Airlines. I've updated my resumé and all the turboprop time looks good. They've lowered their vision requirements and want to interview me. No more night flying for me, if I get the job.

Sometimes it is better not to know what lies ahead.
Note: Much of my career at Northwest Airlines was spent flying on the "back side of the clock"—even worse than flying nights!

My twenty-fifth birthday party in Portland, Oregon
before moving to Minnesota for Northwest Airlines.

Driving down the Columbia Gorge from Boise, Idaho.
The desolation I used to hate driving past is now my home.
You plan, God laughs.

HONESTY

Interviewing for airlines was an experience I'll never forget. I was called to interview for Air California, along with another Forest Service pilot, Dawn. We knew we didn't meet their minimum qualifications, but if they wanted to fly us to southern California for the weekend, who were we to turn them down? Besides, since when do airlines call you? The only drawback was that Air California didn't fly out of Boise, Idaho.

We hopped in Dawn's car and headed for Portland. Interstate 84 is freeway all the way, and she was going over one hundred miles an hour. Dawn said she never got speeding tickets… that she always talked her way out of them. "Well, here's your chance!" I quipped, looking at the flashing lights behind us.

We pulled over and I watched the officer get out of his patrol car. I swear I saw smoke coming out of his ears as he stomped up to Dawn's window. "You ladies better both have flying licenses or you're going to get one hell of a ticket," he said.

We whipped out our FAA licenses and handed them over. He didn't know what to do. The look on his face was hilarious. Scratching his head as he handed them back, he said, "I'm going to have to get a new line."

He let us go, with a serious warning to slow down or else. We laughed the rest of the way to California. I wasn't laughing after my job interview. Flying back on the airplane together, Dawn and I compared notes. Air California wanted to hire us, but we didn't have enough jet time. They told us to come back in a week with 1000 hours. Naively, I responded that there was no way I could fly that much in a week. "Don't you have a pen?" their chief pilot asked.

He wanted me to pencil in jet time? My logbook was sacred—almost like a Bible. There was no way in hell I would contaminate it with P-51 time—pilot lingo for Parker-penned hours. I shook my head.

"Then start another logbook," he said. "Lots of guys do it." He also told me I needed a first class medical with no restrictions. I shook my head again. "I have 20/30 vision and an astigmatism. There's no way I can get that." He handed me the number of a doctor they used who would give me one!

Dawn and I were in agreement. We weren't going to compromise our standards for anyone. Our integrity and honesty were worth more than that. Our eyes were wide open as we headed home.

Sure enough, Northwest Airlines hired me as a flight engineer on the Boeing 727 two weeks later. I knew I would miss the camaraderie and friendships I'd made in Boise, but I was thrilled to be hired as an airline pilot.

Draw your lines in the sand and don't cross them.

I was young and naive, but not stupid.

NEW HIRES

Unbelievable. I made it. I was on cloud ten. There were sixteen of us in Northwest's orientation class, as eager and excited as children at a carnival. This was what we'd all been reaching for: an airline job. *Except for me.* But they'd changed the eye requirements and wanted to hire qualified females. So I was in!

Major airlines are the career pinnacle—what every pilot aspires to. Well, every pilot except for those who don't get hired. You'll hear them talking about "high paid bus drivers" and "wouldn't be caught dead in a boring job like that," but you know it's sour grapes. Busting our asses for years, working for free just to build time, flying for small outfits, and working odd hours—we were all ready for a real job.

Just getting past the initial interviews was hard enough. I was scrutinized, poked, and prodded by Rochester's Mayo Clinic for three days with three other new hires. Doctors checked my blood, my eyes, my heart, my brain, my lungs, my kidneys, and every other organ in my body. *Twice.* I took a written test called the Stanine and had a psychological examination with inkblots. I flew a Boeing 727 simulator, took a written test on basic flying rules, and met with the chief pilots. But I made it, and at least two of the faces in my class were familiar from Mayo Clinic.

When Northwest Airlines hired me, I had 1910 hours in my logbook. The instructor had each of us summarize our flying experience. I was worried about being a token. *What if I had less flight time than the men?* Some of the guys had 3000 hours; some had

1000. I was right in the middle. *What if I'm the only one who needs glasses?* The lights went out and half the class put on their glasses. Northwest was finding it difficult to find pilots with 20/20 vision, so they lowered the requirements to 20/70.

Indoctrination filled the first few weeks, followed by weeks of study on the Boeing 727 systems. We studied fuel, engines, navigation, pressurization, electrical, fire protection, and de-icing systems. We almost learned to *build* the airplane. None of us wanted to bust out. Some people in the class were really stressed, and would never go out to unwind. One student studied every night until three a.m., got a few hours of sleep, and then studied until class started.

The rest of us needed our breaks. One of the guys was our party leader and he set up our weekly drinking sessions. Being from Edina, he knew all the hot spots. The motto back then was that you couldn't fly with the eagles if you can't party with the owls.

One of our classmates couldn't pass the written tests and they had to fire him. I should have been scared, but I was still a bit cavalier about the job. Check rides and tests didn't bother me at all. My mom used to take my brother and me down to her work, where she had lots of games and tests that she used to assess children who were deaf. We were her guinea pigs, and we loved it.

United Airlines had called me for an interview years before when I had only four hundred hours. I knew they wouldn't hire me, but it was good experience. They had a machine they used to measure reaction time. When the light came on, there were a series of steps to turn it off. It was a five-minute test, but mine kept going. And going. Finally, I looked at the tester and asked him how long it had been. "Twenty minutes. I've never seen anyone do this well," he admitted, "and I just wanted to see if you could keep it up. Can you go faster?" I didn't think I could without introducing mistakes, but I tried. It was fun, and so was this 727 training program at Northwest.

We flew to Dallas to use Braniff's simulators since ours were full. Our instructors let us know right off the bat that if we didn't party with them, we wouldn't make it through training. We studied constantly, and the simulator sessions were intense. I was still having fun, but I was working hard and having to prove myself to some of the instructors who didn't think a female could grasp the technical systems. One of them told me I had it out and was stepping on it. I told him I didn't have one so I couldn't be stepping on it.

Two months later I took my check ride. I remember walking into a pitch black cockpit. We were taught not to turn the power on until we did our "safety check." It would be easy to injure a mechanic if they were working on the plane. When I turned my flashlight on, I saw two nearly-naked men in the captain and copilot seat. The support guys were joking around and sitting in the dark in their underwear. It broke the tension for me and I relaxed.

The examiner was furious. This was serious business and we were not supposed to be having fun. For two hours I worked through problems and I thought my checkride was over. Instead we went back in for two more hours because the man claimed he couldn't get the simulator to work right. The guys up front were getting bored, so they were flying through high-rises and skimming along the ground. Finally the checkride was over.

The support crew left, congratulating me on their way out. I thought we were going to go to a debriefing room. Instead the examiner put us "back in the air." He told me he hadn't seen me do a "climb flow." I told him that was because I hadn't seen a climb. I was tired and angry. My check ride was over five hours. What started as a fun night was now a nightmare. Finally, the examiner passed me. It turned out that he was nervous about a female flight engineer being good enough to "fly his family."

Life isn't fair. Get over it.

I'm checked out on the Boeing 727 as a flight engineer, or second officer, as we were also called.

I'M A GIRL

After months of training with Northwest—in the classroom, simulator, and the airplane—I was ready to fly on my own, without an instructor. I lived close to the airport because I was a little *too* conscientious. Crew scheduling called me for my first trip, and it was scheduled to leave in three hours. Excitedly, I asked the scheduler what to do next, because the flight time was so close to the call time. Exasperated, she told me, "Just show up an hour before."

I packed my bag and put on my uniform. It took me less than an hour to get ready, so I was at the airport an hour and fifty minutes early. When I walked up to the check-in window the scheduler I talked to earlier said, "You're a no show. You've been replaced."

I was in shock. The smile on my face changed to disbelief. All the blood drained out of my head. "How? When? Why?"

"You didn't make your two-hour call," she says smugly.

First I was scared and then I was mad. "Of course I didn't. You called me. I was on my way. You said to just show up."

"You still have to make your two-hour call. You're a no-show," she shouted out over her shoulder, walking back to her desk.

"Now what do I do?" I asked in frustration.

"Go home. Wait for us to call you again. Do it right. Or you can go see the chief pilot now… *The Man in the Empty Suit.*"

She was laughing as I walked away. I found out later that she couldn't stand the thought of female pilots on her turf.

I barely knew what a Boeing 727 was before I was checked out to fly on it!

We were a threat… competition, because she and her girlfriend dated the pilots. How had I not noticed that being a female in this career was not going to be easy? I was so naive.

I went to the chief pilot's office. He was incredulous. "How could they write you up as a no show when there is still an hour and forty-five minutes before your flight?" he asked. I agreed. I didn't understand either. He chuckled and told me not to worry about it; just don't get in any more trouble.

Honestly, I was a little paranoid that first year. I should have realized how hard this career was going to be and how easily my career could be over. First my awful check ride. Then the no show. There were so many rules. I was beginning to care too much about the airline career.

Crew scheduling called me for all the short-notice trips the first year and a half. Other than short calls, I didn't fly until late in the month, after the guys in my class had full schedules. Crew scheduling gave them the best trips; I got the leftovers. I bought a house in Minnesota less than ten minutes from the airport. Come sleet, hail or dead of night, nothing was going to keep me from my appointed flights. I never understood why pilots complicated their lives by commuting. Northwest would never have to worry about me being late for work ever again.

After our probation party at the end of the year, I began to relax, even though I still had a few months to go. All the guys were telling stories of mistakes they had made the first year. One of the guys had imbalanced the fuel by 7,000 pounds, quite a lot on a Boeing 727. He was cocky, by his own admission, chastising the pilots for their lack of skill when they complained the plane was "wing heavy." Then the captain noticed the fuel gages. The fuel was barely balanced within legal limits before landing. The captain never wrote him up.

One of my classmates took more time to get dressed than his girlfriend, according to her. He didn't want to get his hair wet on rainy days, so, instead of doing a preflight, he stood under the jetway stairs, "preflighting" the airplane from there. An instructor caught him in the act and told him that he'd better have everything else up to snuff or he was gone. *Uh oh.* My classmate had left his tools and required manuals at home because they were too heavy. He still passed.

Another guy was too drunk to fly, so crew scheduling moved on to the next name on the list. He wasn't written up, either. He was dating one of the crew schedulers. *Why didn't I think of that?*

When I went in for my probationary interview, I wasn't worried. I had done nothing wrong all year. The captains I flew with gave me great reviews and all the paperwork was positive. The assistant chief pilot said everything looked great. "Welcome to Northwest! You made it off probation!" Then he noticed something in my folder. "Wait a minute. You have a no-show here."

I explained the circumstances and he was surprised. A watch had been placed on me the first six months and there was no explanation or reason given. I realized my "no-show" was a big deal after all. Now I knew why the chief pilot was called *The Man in the Empty Suit.* He wouldn't take a stand. Some of my paranoia returned. I was just lucky nothing else had gone wrong.

For the most part, being accepted was easier than I expected. I was a flight engineer on the Boeing 727 for the first three years. It was funny to see the pilots' reactions to having a female in the cockpit. "Oh my gosh. A girl. I thought I'd never live to see the day." Then they would watch me like a hawk until they were satisfied I could do the job. Or nitpick me to death until I couldn't. But as soon as the men discovered that I was qualified and good at my job, there was no problem. In fact, I was treated like a queen. Many of the captains bought me dinner and drinks, despite my protests. There were very few inappropriate advances. The men who were jerks to me were jerks to the male pilots as well.

I knew being accepted at an airline might be difficult. One of the airline captains hired to fly with us in the Learjet had told me to keep my mouth shut and my hands to myself. He pulled out his Penthouse and Playboy magazines and did his best to make me uncomfortable. Going into Salt Lake City, he was on final without getting a landing clearance. I wasn't allowed to talk to him or to the controllers. Every time I opened my mouth he told me to shut up. Finally, I blurted out, "Fine, land without a clearance." He treated me a little better after that, but not much.

There was pornography at Northwest, too, but being offended wasn't an option. It was, after all, a man's job. I thought it was funny how much was hidden underneath desktops and inside the smoke rope door, just for shock appeal. So I started hiding my own... but only naked guys instead of naked women. Both sexes could play this game. When the worst offenders realized I wasn't going to turn them in to the chief pilot, it made being accepted as "one of the guys" that much easier. The atmosphere became more congenial, and if the jokes got too graphic, I just turned around and tuned them out.

***It is a good thing I didn't know how hard being a
female airline pilot was going to be.***

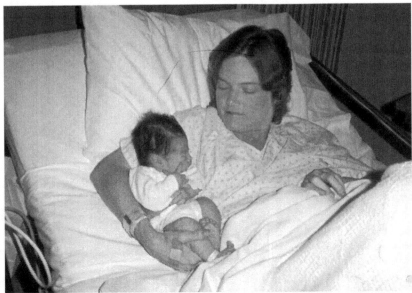

Does it get any better than this?

PREGNANT

My uniform was getting tight. There were no maternity pants or shirts. Northwest Airlines had never had a pregnant pilot before. It was unheard of! Un-thought of! The captains and copilots were trying to carry my bags for me and offering to do my preflight. "I'm not sick. I'm just pregnant. I'm probably healthier than you are. I can carry my bags—I lift weights and do aerobics every day. I'm fine," I assured them.

And I was. I'd wake up early in my hotel room and eat just enough crackers to throw up. That was usually all the morning sickness I had. Once, and only once, I raced up the aft airstairs of the 727 during my preflight and threw up in the back lavatory sink. Other than that, I had no trouble doing my job.

Still, at five and a half months I decided to look into other alternatives. I knew pilots on medical leave were allowed to work in the simulators—in other words, they filled an empty seat and participated in training exercises and check rides for pay. I talked to Charlie Lindberg in administration about my dilemma. He called the training department. Yes, they told him, they could use me as a panel-watcher—a flight engineer in the simulator—three or four days a month.

That wasn't enough for a full schedule, so I opted to keep flying. "But you can't. You don't have a maternity uniform," Charlie said.

I wasn't backing down. "They didn't have a female pilot uniform when I started and you had me buy navy blue pants at J.C.

Penney. I'll buy a pair of navy maternity pants and sew my epaulets on a white maternity top. It will look fine."

Charlie almost had a heart attack. *A maternity uniform for a pilot?* He said he would make a few more calls and sort things out. At home the next morning my phone rang. It was Charlie. "We can fill you up in training," he said. Jubilation! Now I could feel like a professional again and do my job.

I loved panel watching. Every instructor had different ideas, and I learned something new all the time. I got better and better at handling "emergencies." Certain instructors were my favorites, and one of them, Gary Thompson, warned me that he was going to turn off the dampener so the student could see how bad his landings *really* were. We bounced seven times down the runway. My baby woke up and starting kicking me. That got a laugh out of everyone and the student learned his lesson.

Nothing is ever as easy as it seems. One of the instructors overheard me talking about seat belts in cars during pregnancy doing more harm than good, and that you were almost better off not to wear one, because all the blood flow to the uterus meant that you could easily bleed to death before help arrived. I should have kept my mouth shut.

This instructor didn't want me in training to begin with, and he had been impossible to work with. He thought women were an annoyance—he didn't believe a woman could perform a job as important as being a pilot. He kicked me out of the simulator. Then he went to the head of training, Don Juries, and told him I wouldn't wear my seatbelt—an FAA rule, even in the simulator.

I was called into Don's office. That wasn't what had happened, I told him, and related the incident. Don laughed, told me to wear my seatbelt, and that was the end of it. The best part was that I didn't have to fly with that instructor ever again.

When I was nine and a half months along, one of the simulator instructors asked, "When *are* you going to have that baby?" We were circling near Chicago, in a phantom holding pattern.

"Soon," I answered, "I've had labor pains all morning."

The guys panicked, and wanted to land immediately. I reminded them we weren't really in the air flying over Chicago. Besides, our training facility was only a few miles from my hospital. They relaxed. *A little.* They still took the simulator off motion and made me leave for the hospital as soon as the training session was over. There wasn't any hurry. I was still in labor thirty hours later.

You can have it all. If you have seniority.

Darcie at age three.

My divorce cake.

Darcie and I all dressed up at home in Minnesota.

DIVORCE

My marriage of ten years was disintegrating. *At last.* I realized it wasn't all my fault and the problems were way bigger than me. I had been too stubborn to quit. Our road had been a rocky one. My husband and I would fight; he would move out. Then he would apologize, and we would get back together again a few months later. I joked that I should have a revolving door installed so that he could come and go as he pleased. The last time he had moved back in was three weeks before Christmas. His father came for the holidays and that was the last straw.

We had a huge fight after my father-in-law left. I was sure my husband's father had been inappropriate with our daughter. My husband disagreed. "For better or for worse" did not mean staying in a bad marriage. Our values were at opposite ends of the spectrum, and we didn't want the same things in life. I filed for divorce and moved on with my life.

I started seeing a counselor, and went to an Adult Children of Alcoholics group in St. Paul. I took my daughter to a counselor who assured me that, all in all, Darcie is a well-adjusted little girl. Most parents, she said, never see what is happening until it is too late. What mom wouldn't let a grandpa take a child for ice cream or to the playground? I still blamed myself, but the counselor said abusers are incredibly calculating and careful, and that I should be patting myself on the back for stopping the abuse.

My job as a mother was to protect my child. I had failed. The guilt I feel is sometimes overwhelming.

Hindsight is 20/20. I couldn't agree more.

Introducing Darcie to the cockpit.

COMMUTING

When I had my daughter I had enough seniority to be home every day and my husband was there nights. I could nurse her, put her in bed for the night, fly to Kansas City and be back in time for her morning feeding. Yes, I had it all figured out and I was pretty smug about it.

I swore I would never be a commuter. Living close to the airport was the ticket for my peace of mind. I upgraded to flight engineer on the DC10, with layovers in Honolulu and Fort Lauderdale. Escaping Minnesota winters, even for a day, was a coup. I was chosen to be a line instructor, giving initial operating experience to new flight engineers.

A year later I checked out as copilot on the 727. It felt great to have a real flying seat again; to actually do the takeoffs and landings. The trouble was, being a copilot I had to prove myself all over again. Being a flight engineer was one thing—a secretarial job of sorts, in their minds, keeping the logbook and the pay sheet. Besides, I was sitting *behind* them. Flying every other takeoff and landing, being a real "co" pilot, did not sit well with some of the captains.

It seemed that one month would be good, the next one would be bad. I knew I could fly an airplane, and I didn't have trouble with my check rides, but I was a threat. Having to prove myself every time I stepped into a cockpit was getting old. Even after proving I could do a good job, the hassles continued.

I was descending into Detroit at 260 knots. The captain took the airplane away from me and pasted the passengers on the ceiling. He literally yanked the plane up to slow it down ten knots. "When Detroit says they want 250 knots, then they want 250 knots."

I was shocked. Luckily no one was injured. The flight attendants were furious. They couldn't stand the captain. The rest of the trip went downhill from there. The flight engineer didn't like the man either, and neither did other copilots. I decided I would never fly with him again, for safety reasons. Because I loved to fly, it was worth putting up with the bad months. I didn't realize how much I had missed takeoffs and landings, talking on the radio, and navigating. It was so much fun! I swore I would never fly as a flight engineer again. Then I started dating a man who lived in eastern Oregon.

I taught Kevin to fly years before, and he contacted me about continuing his training. He had been farming the family land and loved it, but his blood pressure was up because he couldn't get all the tractor work done in a timely manner. Frustrated, unable to do his job well, he was quitting and moving to Portland. He decided the Twin Cities (Minneapolis/St. Paul) would work just as well when we started dating seriously.

His uncles realized he was going to leave and didn't want to see him go. They talked to his partner and made some big changes in the workload distribution so Kevin would stay. I realized he would never leave the ranch. I didn't know what to do.

I had never considered commuting. I knew I didn't want to be a flight engineer, nor did I want to be away from my daughter for long periods of time. But I was in love and I was the only one who could make it work for both of us. So I upgraded to a position on the 747 as flight engineer. I moved to a wheat ranch in Oregon and commuted to Minneapolis, Los Angeles, Seattle, and Anchorage. There are pilots with worse commutes, like the Phillipines or Spain, but mine is complicated enough for me.

I swore I would never be a commuter
or fly as flight engineer again.
Now I swear to never swear.

I married Kevin in 1988 and moved to eastern Oregon.
The middle of nowhere… the toolies… the boondocks.

Our spring wheat under the wind towers.

Antelope not only play, they reproduce like rabbits!

HOME ON THE RANGE

What in God's name was I doing out here in the middle of nowhere? Never in my wildest dreams did I imagine that my life and my home would be so far from anywhere. *Okay, maybe in my wildest dreams. There were those high school plans that included marrying a Montana sheep rancher.* But here? Near the end of the Oregon Trail surrounded by dry land wheat fields, nothingness, and wind? Never. I did want to live on the Oregon Coast when I visited the Northwest in college, but that was three and a half hours away.

Our house is ten miles from the nearest town of four hundred people. It's a hundred and fifty miles from the Pacific Ocean. "We live in the boondocks," my daughter said. Some days, when the wind is blowing at seventy miles an hour or more, even my husband can't fathom what we're doing living here. He cursed the wind and claimed there was no reason for it to blow this hard. I explained the Venturi Principle, how the Columbia Gorge narrows, creating a pressure differential, then widens near our ranch. "Don't you remember me teaching you that years ago, when you were learning how to fly?" He gave me *the look*.

"Don't blame yourself. Blame your ancestors," I admonished. "They're the idiots who stopped here. They could have followed the Barlow Toll Road just a little farther to the end of the trail." We could be living in the lush Willamette River Valley south of Portland where it rains more than ten inches annually and the rich soil produces three harvests a year. We're lucky to get forty bushels every other year. Or they could have stopped farther east. The land upriver near the Idaho border known as *Palouse Country* has crops of 120 bushels per acre. Even a few miles south there is less wind.

An hour farther west, the Columbia Gorge is a beautiful place where waterfalls cascade down rocky cliffs and mossy rocks and ferns abound. Pine and fruit trees line the hillsides and the views are awe-inspiring. Just west of our exit on the freeway a sign proclaims: Now leaving the Scenic Columbia Gorge. As in, arriving at the *un-scenic* part. "The face of the moon," a friend of ours calls it. On windy days my lungs are filled with dust and my contact lenses turn my eyes into red holes. This is surely hell.

We visited my husband's roots in Killen, Scotland in 1995. Great great great great grandfather Archibald Macnab's picture still hangs in the Killen tavern with the family tartan carpeting the floor. The old scoundrel fathered over seventy children. Yes, seventy! You either loved or hated the man, they said. Obviously, the women loved him. After all these generations, my husband and his uncles still look a little like the red bearded Macnab on the family crest. The Macnabs were run out of Scotland by the Campbells... as in Campbell's soup Campbells, I suppose. They escaped to Canada, then homesteaded Oregon in the 1800s. Except for lupine on the hills instead of heather, our part of the gorge looks like northern Scotland. It is barren and rocky and God-forsaken, but it must have reminded them of home.

The Van Pattens homesteaded the land our house is on, having married into the Macnabs. Their primary goal was to get a crop planted. That explains why there's a house out here on this dusty stretch of prairie that is almost desert. Oregon's Homestead Act proclaimed that you must sleep and eat on your land, so two cousins and two brothers built one house on their adjoining four corners of land. Each corner had a bed and table. They were Dutch, so they were conserving their resources in order to plant sooner. Rumor has it you were supposed to have glass in your windows. Pane glass broke too easily and was hard to come by. Instead they each drank a pint of whiskey and placed the empty bottle in the windows. Five years later the land was officially theirs.

My mother-in-law and her siblings were raised in this house. Her brothers remember *shoveling* out the living room for their mother after a dust storm. That was after they moved out of the house for three days because they couldn't breathe. Good old Oregon top soil. Thank goodness there's a lot of it because every year it sandblasts the sides of our home.

When I first moved here the siding and windows were little better than a tar paper shack. Okay, I'm exaggerating a little, but not by much. Pink asphalt siding covered the original wood and tar paper to slow the wind down. There was pane glass in the windows, albeit cheap, single panes. The windowsills had an inch of dirt on them, the dishes in the cupboard: just under a half inch. I had to vacuum the windowsills daily, but at least I didn't need a shovel.

Growing up, my chore was to dust the house once a month, whether it needed it or not. Forests of trees held down the soil in Florida and the windows were closed because we had air conditioning. Now I understood why people had to dust. Determined not to spend my days cleaning, I hired a siding contractor to insulate the house, put on new vinyl siding, and install double pane windows. To me these were necessities.

Our biggest marital fight was over air conditioning. My husband had a blanket and a window air conditioner in the living room and couldn't understand why I needed central air when it only got over a hundred degrees a few weeks in the summer. His relatives thought I was an idiot. Who spent thousands of dollars on a house they didn't own, and why was I spending all his money? I avoided all controversy by avoiding the naysayers until one morning. Kevin's Uncle Pat decided to visit the house.

"I would never let my wife work. Never," he declared as I set a cup of coffee in front of him.

I smiled. To fit in, I knew I needed to keep my mouth shut, especially around Uncle Pat. This is the man who hides his money under his mattress and walks around nude in his yard. He doesn't believe in the Holocaust and he thinks Hollywood set up the moon landing.

"I just don't know what's wrong with Kevin, letting you work." He gulps his coffee and waits for me to take the bait.

Are you kidding me? I work to stay sane! I didn't answer.

"Jeeze, for a lousy ten thousand a year. Leaving your husband and kids…" He shakes his head.

"Well, I make more than that," I reply, unable to keep my mouth shut any longer. I glance at the back door, praying for my husband to come rescue me from this conversation.

"I wouldn't have let Maxine work for twenty thousand. No siree."

He probably thinks a woman's place is home with her family, not gallivanting all over the world. "Well, I make a little more than that." I sipped my coffee and settled into the conversation. Now I was having fun.

"Or at least work closer to home. Horizon, what about them? Alaska Airlines? Why do you have to fly off to Japan? No siree, I wouldn't let her work for thirty thousand, either."

"Not even close," I answer, smiling.

Archibald Macnab

I can't imagine twelve children growing up in our small, three-bedroom farm house!

"Forty?" His coffee cup is frozen in midair, shaking, making whitecaps on his coffee.

I do a thumbs up. "Higher."

"Fifty?"

I shake my head.

He's shocked. Stunned. "Damn. I would have let Maxine work every day of the year for seventy thousand." He walks out, shaking his head in disbelief.

Yes, Uncle Pat, women can make good money in this world. Seventy thousand? Where did he come up with that figure? Has anyone ever left Uncle Pat speechless? Yes. Finally. Me. Kathy Last Word. My mother would be proud.

Half an hour later his youngest son stopped by. Harry was in stitches, laughing. "What did you say to Dad? He stumbled into the house, shaking his head and moaning, 'Seventy thousand a year. Damn. Seventy thousand.' Then he plopped into his chair, muttering and shaking his head."

"Yeah, he came over for coffee and kept badgering me about what I make."

"But you make double that," Harry said.

"He was so stunned that I was afraid to tell him what I really made... I would have given him a heart attack."

Life on the farm is never boring. I mean, life on the *ranch*. My mother looked up the definition in her dictionary and informed us that a ranch is an extensive farm devoted to one crop. I think Mom wanted to tell her friends that her daughter married a rancher.

Kevin calls it a farm. He says he's a dirt farmer and that ranches have animals—sheep, cows, etc. Kevin doesn't do animals—working on a pig farm in fifth grade convinced him that animals were too much work. My parents were at our house watching Darcie while we were on vacation when my mom noticed cows in the yard. "Oh, Kevin's cows are out," Mom said. My daughter, four at the time, took her thumb out of her mouth long enough to say, "Kebin don't hab no cows."

The pilots I fly with are envious. "You must have a great ranch house if they homesteaded there. Is it huge?" I try not to laugh. Twelve children were raised in my tiny house, and the square footage is less than a thousand feet. The boys slept on a sleeping porch that became my daughter's bedroom. There was a bedroom for the girls and one for the parents. The bathroom was an outhouse. They added a living room in the 1930s for $500.

Winter nights when we put together jigsaw puzzles or play cards I can almost hear Kevin's ancestors laughing and talking. They used to pop corn over the open fire and play ping pong on a piece of plywood Grandma Bee placed on the dining table. The house was cozy and comfortable now, but I still felt like a pioneer.

The uncles and aunts started making regular visits. They entered, often without knocking, which was fine with me. I enjoyed following them as they reminisced, trying to see the place through their eyes. "I swear, this house seemed bigger when we were growing up," Uncle Pete says.

I'm sure it did. *They were children.* Now the uncles stand over six feet tall and have to duck through some of the doorways. There were eight boys. Six of them served in World War II and they all made it home. Uncle Tom was down to eighty pounds after starving in the swamps of New Guinea and suffering from malaria. Cousin Bill was killed instantly when his B-17 collided with another B-17 near Hamburg, Germany in 1944.

"Remember when this bedroom was a sleeping porch, waking up, covered with snow?" Tom asked, shivering.

Pete nodded. "Remember the icicles? You could see your breath."

One of the boys, Johnny, tripped and discharged a shotgun through the kitchen floor. He evaded his mother's wrath by pulling the throw rug over the hole and moving the table—until she went downstairs to bring up a jar of jam from the cellar. Broken glass was everywhere.

A double-hole outhouse seat propped against the barn wall reminds me that not too long ago, in a windstorm or a blizzard, going outside was a necessity. The uncles delighted in hiding in the dark, leaping out of the shadows to toss clawing, wild kittens on their shrieking, terrified sisters. Until the day they died, the girls were afraid of cats.

Kevin's mom remembered windblown drifts of snow so high that "Daddy had to get the horses out to take us to the one room schoolhouse." Today, we *occasionally* have enough snow to sled on, but it's not like the old days.

Rose and Helen remembered dresses made from potato sacks and being thankful for them. They hauled water by hand up the canyon in buckets. The same water was used first for cooking, then for washing dishes, then clothes, bathing, and at last for watering the rose bushes. I can only marvel at their tenacity as I push buttons to run my dishwasher.

My well is six hundred feet deep, with a flow of only ten gallons per minute, but the water is pure and good.

Uncle Pat used to joke with Rose. "Remember when we shot you playing cowboys and Indians out in the old barn? We left you for dead and ran for the house. Didn't think Mom would miss

"Kebin don't hab no cows."

Van Patten barn out my front window.

one… Then you wandered in, half an hour later, bleeding and bawling your head off. Got us into a lot of trouble, you did," Pat said, as if it were Rose's fault.

My mother-in-law would nod. Of course she remembered. The bullet went in through her jaw and out her cheek, and gave her problems with her teeth forever. At least her brothers and cousins received the whipping they deserved.

Oh, and the old chicken coop still standing by the barn? The chickens used to have gold in their gullets, so some of the uncles were convinced there was a cache somewhere. They kept their mineral rights when they sold us land, just in case we discover gold someday.

Today, our gold is in the form of wind power. Portland General Electric built wind towers on our land. We could still farm around the towers and finally, the wind became a blessing instead of a curse. We didn't have to worry as much about having a good crop. With an average rainfall of seven to eleven inches a year, it is shocking that anything will grow. I know. I tried for ten years to grow a garden—mostly I grew big weeds. How my husband can plant and harvest four thousand acres of wheat is beyond me.

The Oregon Trail ran right through our property. Believe it or not, we can still see the wagon ruts in some of our fields in the spring as the new shoots of wheat push skyward—that's how deep they were. As solitary as life is here, I find it hard to imagine the thousands of people that came by on their way west. Our nearest neighbor is a mile away.

I rise each morning to the crowing of pheasants and I fall asleep to the howling of coyotes. Meadowlarks sing their songs; deer and antelope abound. You've never seen a lawn as big as ours—thousands of acres of lush green, soft white winter wheat. Morning and evening walks smell like fresh bread baking as the wheat turns golden in the late spring.

There's nothing better than relaxing in my Jacuzzi under millions of stars, listening to coyotes howl. This land is so vast and so open that it reminds me of the Utah desert. When I worked at the coal mine in southern Utah, sometimes my shift finished at midnight and I couldn't fly out until the next morning. I would throw my sleeping bag on the ground and sleep under a canopy of stars. (Later I learned there were tiny white scorpions and rattlesnakes that inhabited the desert there, but at the time I slept like a baby.)

"This must be so boring for you, living here after traveling all over the world," my neighbors remark when I am home. Boring? Never. Solace. An oasis. Here, miles from everywhere, I can forget the beggars in Bangkok and the polluted skies of China. Asia, with its hordes of people, is a mere memory. We truly are in the middle of nowhere. The toolies. The boondocks. Our life is simple, our wants, few. Sunrises are fantastic… sunsets over Mount Hood are amazing. I love my home sweet home on the range.

Captain Tom Genz used to tell me:

"Be careful what you wish for—you just might get it."

Colt with a calf. Still bigger than he is.

My girlfriend lets us play with her cows!

PEOPLE PROBLEMS

S itting in my office, watching the world go by six miles below is amazing. The panoramic view up front is not the same as the one in the passenger seats. It's not boring, although it can be better or worse depending who you are flying with. There are always little mechanical problems to solve, but most of the time it is routine. Usually we laugh and joke, or solve each other's problems. Sometimes we ponder why in the world a nautical term like *cockpit*, with no sexual innuendo at all, is now called the flight deck.

I got up to stretch my legs one day while crossing the Pacific. It was dark and all the lights were out so that passengers could sleep and watch movies. I almost tripped over a lady stretched out in the aisle. She gave me a dirty look. I walked around her to the galley and asked the flight attendants about her.

"She won't move. She says her back hurts," one of the flight attendants said, rolling her eyes.

"Do you want her there?" I asked.

"Are you kidding? She wouldn't even move during our snack service. It's unsafe because it's hard to see her in the dark, until you trip over her. Can you get her to move?"

"Of course." *No problem. This was going to be fun.* I walked back and accidentally tripped over her.

"Ow. Watch where you're going, Bitch."

"Ma'am, you're going to have to move out of the aisle and into your seat."

"No. My back hurts and this is a long flight."

"Everyone's back hurts and you don't see everyone else sitting in the aisle. Walk around or stand back by the lavatories but get up out of the aisle."

"What gives you the authority to boss me around?"

"These do," I say, pointing to my epaulets. She changes tactics and starts telling me how badly the flight attendants have treated her. "It's because you are in their way while they're trying to do their job," I explain.

"They wouldn't even give me a snack."

She sounded like a pouty two-year-old, but she's well over forty-one... one of the "me-first" generation. "That's because you're in their way. If you get in your seat, you might get served." I'm losing my patience with her fast.

"I'll just get back in the aisle after you leave," she says defiantly, moving into her seat.

"Then we'll have the authorities meet the flight and escort you to jail for disobeying us." This was fun. I can still be a bit of a brat when pushed, and I have a two-year-old at home that she reminds me of. She argues a little longer, but doesn't leave her seat.

I ask the flight attendants later in the flight, "Did she ever get back in the aisle?"

"Not after you talked to her. Thanks! Now we know who to ask when we need help."

ANOTHER TIME ONE of our baggage handlers traveling on a pass was harassing the flight attendants. I learned his name, where he was from, and what his job was with the company by communicating with the departure station by radio. Then I went back to deal with him. He was belligerent and self-important, trying to get moved up to first class. He was indignant because the flight attendant wouldn't serve him free booze. I informed him that he could lose his pass privileges forever if he didn't apologize and mind his manners.

"Oh yeah, who's going to do that? You don't even know me." He sat back smugly in his seat.

"Well *John*, I will have law enforcement meet this flight and you can find your own way back to Los Angeles for work on Monday, if you still have a job."

The look on his face was priceless. He had no clue we could look him up in the system to see who he was, and fell all over himself groveling and then apologizing, swearing never to act up again.

WE'VE ALWAYS TAKEN security incidents seriously. A man on our flight to Honolulu was being lewd, crude, and a real pain in the ass. He was lifting passenger's dresses and touching them inappropriately. Everyone around him was fed up, and it was a six-hour flight from hell. We warned him, but nothing helped. So, we had the FBI meet the aircraft.

Deplaning, the man was sure he was home free. Lifting a lady's dress above her head he taunted, "Woo hoo, look at this!" as he stepped out onto the jetway. A waiting FBI agent grabbed his raised arm and spun him around so hard we could hear his head whack the side of the plane, breaking his nose. Everyone cheered. There is justice in the world!

PEOPLE DO ALMOST anything when they think there are no conse-quences. I love having some power. But so often it seems that noth-ing comes of an incident and it is frustrating to know that jerks have gotten away with bad behavior. The flight attendants com-plained about one woman in particular, the wife of an oil sheik, who had actually punched one of them in the nose and slapped another. Her kids were separated from her, and she was handcuffed to a seat.

"Just wait until my husband hears about the way I've been treated. He'll have you all fired," she threatened.

Months later there had never been any follow up. Not another word. The flight attendants were angry about the company never taking their side. They complained at our annual training in Minneapolis and the instructor promised to look into the incident. After the break, he told us what he had learned.

"Her husband had her *beheaded* when she returned to Saudi Arabia. She had embarrassed him with her behavior one too many times."

A hush came over the room. The flight attendants involved were horrified. It had never occurred to them that this proud, haughty woman with two children would be *killed* for misbehaving. They felt guilty for writing up the incident.

Just when I thought nothing could surprise me…

COPILOT CHECKOUT

It had been a long month flying on IOE, or what our company called initial operating experience. I'd watched a hundred guys go through the process. I had even *given* IOE to flight engineers as an IOE instructor. But I had never seen anyone treated the way this captain instructor was treating me. I was doing a good job as copilot, but his constant nitpicking was taking its toll. At least I wouldn't have to fly with him again. He had signed me off and this was my last landing with him.

Los Angeles Approach gave us traffic at twelve o'clock. We couldn't find it. We finally saw the other plane, but by that time I needed to go around because I was too high. The captain wouldn't let me, because he didn't want to miss his commuter flight home. I told him it was his airplane because I wasn't comfortable being this high. He said that if I wanted to be signed off, I had to fly it.

Damn him. I got back on glideslope, but I was still too fast. The left wing did a huge dip just as I pulled the power off all the way on landing. I recovered, but I didn't feel good about it.

"Now you've got the bad one out of the way," he quipped, with an unreadable expression on his face. I looked down at the rudder trim as we were taxiing in. It was set at three. I had never seen it out of detente except in the simulator during engine failures. I looked at the instructor in disbelief and pointed. Looking down, he stuttered, "What? I didn't do that."

The flight attendant even asked us about the landing and the dip of the wing tip. "I've never felt that before," he said, "Kind of scary." I was too angry to answer. The captain handed me my signed off paperwork and said, "Congratulations."

I returned home lacking the elation I should have felt after being signed off to fly as copilot. I called scheduling to tell them I was released for line flying. Scheduling said "No, your instructor didn't sign you off."

I called the instructor captain at home and asked what was going on. Stuttering again, he said there were too many inept captains out there to have a weak copilot.

I was stunned. I told him it shouldn't affect my checkout if there were captains who weren't safe, and since when was I weak? I had passed the simulator sessions with flying colors.

He said, "Since that landing in Los Angeles. You need to call the head of training to find out what to do next."

The head of 747 training told me I would be taking my "final" check ride on Saturday out of Honolulu. He said I had exceeded the number of hours I was allowed for initial operating experience. There would be no more chances.

I was angry. "How did I cost the company too much money? I was on my regular schedule! There was no extra money spent on me *at all*. Plus, I just got home. I can't go to Honolulu in three days."

There was a pause before he said, "I strongly suggest you be there. It will be your last chance."

I was paralyzed with fear. Fear of humiliation, fear of failing. Silly in retrospect, but so real at the time. *No pressure*. To this day I remember where was I sitting and what I was feeling as all these thoughts rushed through me. I called my mom, crying. I told her they were trying to bust me out. She calmed me down, telling me they had hassled me on checkouts before. How was this any different?

She was right. Besides, it shouldn't come as any surprise to me that they still didn't want female copilots. The head of ground training had called my house before I started training to tell my husband I wouldn't make it through! *Who does that?* It was just a warning, but perhaps one I should have heeded. Or documented. Friends thought I should sue, or turn the company in for sexual harassment. I knew suing was a recipe for disaster in the years down the road. Good old boys know how to get even.

I told myself that I didn't care. I knew I could do it. They couldn't scare me. But now I realized the deck was stacked and they very well could flunk me. No matter how well I flew, there would always be something I didn't do quite right. Everyone in aviation knows that check rides can be too hard.

Silly, unreal scenarios raced through me. *What will people think of me? They won't want to be friends with a failure. They'll talk about me. 'Did you hear? She couldn't make it. Women shouldn't be pilots.'* It was crazy to be thinking along these lines, but I saw my whole career going up in smoke.

Another voice inside me said, "This is ridiculous. Have any of your friends even tried to be a pilot? The ones who love you won't think anything bad. The rest probably won't even know you failed unless you tell them. None of your friends are friends with you because you're a pilot. They're friends with you because they like you."

I had a few days before my "final" flight. I decided to go to Minneapolis and fly the simulator again, just to bolster my confidence and be prepared. Ron, the simulator instructor, put me through everything he could think of, trying to find something wrong with my technique. He gave me maximum crosswinds from the left and right, precision and non-precision approaches with minimum visibility, then the same approaches with maximum crosswinds and engine failures.

Two hours, later he threw up his hands. "Kath, I just don't see any problems with your flying. I'll call your check airman and tell him I think you're being set up."

Relieved and reassured, I went to Honolulu a day early, determined to do my best. *So what if they didn't pass me? At least I wouldn't give up.* I walked on the beach and went to my favorite restaurant before getting a good night's sleep.

I was in the planning room the next morning, charting our course from Hawaii to Japan, when the instructor showed up. The first thing he said to me after introducing himself was, "Good luck. I've failed more than thirty pilots out of this position."

What the hell? What a jerk. I asked him if Ron had called.

"Yes, he left a message but I didn't call him back. Nothing you did in the simulator could outweigh what your IOE instructor captain already told me."

Fine. So that's the way it's going to play out. Nervous and shaky, I walked to our airplane. I don't fly my best under false, manmade pressure. This wasn't looking good.

There was no camaraderie. He wouldn't answer routine questions. I quickly realized I would be doing his job and mine. With a plane full of 354 passengers, something inside me snapped. The fear left and I just decided to enjoy my last few days flying as copilot.

I took off, climbed out, handled the radios, and did all the navigation by myself. He evaluated. I was too angry and frustrated to talk to him, and of course I wouldn't risk my job by doing anything unrelated to flying. So I read and reread the flight plan, taking note of the radio stations that were out of service in Japan. He made fun of me for writing down the holding fixes on my note pad. "What, you think they're going to give you holding on a clear blue day?" he jeered.

Nearing Tokyo, ATC gave us a clearance to hold at an intersection that was not on the map. This would require using two radio frequencies and mileages that weren't readily available. The intersection was only ten miles away and we were flying at over 500 miles an hour. Panicked, he fumbled for the flight envelope. I had it memorized. "It's nonstandard, twenty-five miles off Onjuku and ten miles off of…"

"Just do it," he interrupted.

I slowed and entered holding at the intersection with a left hand turn. I put in a wind correction, flew the outbound leg, and did a standard rate turn back towards the fix. The needles centered as I flew over the intersection. "That's textbook perfect," he said, in a tone that was incredulous and almost reverent.

Or dumbass luck, I thought, thanking my lucky stars.

His whole demeanor changed. He became helpful and respectful, complimentary and encouraging. He talked to me on approach, giving me tips. My landing was slightly askew… a little crooked. My last instructor berated me for my less than perfect landings, but gave me no instruction to improve them. "Hell, that's all Plat was worried about? This airplane can land in a crab. Just don't start walking the rudders. Let it straighten itself out. It's an old man's airplane, so nothing happens fast."

The next day we flew to Hong Kong's legendary airport in Kowloon—the hardest airport in our system, but also the most fun.

Joking, with him talking me through it, it was almost easy. Using his suggestions, my third landing, back into Narita, Japan, was perfect. *So much for failing.* He signed me off with no reservations.

The irony in all this is that the very instructor who hassled me the most was promoted to a chief pilot position. He was already the head of the sexual harassment committee for ALPA, our pilot union. So who could I talk to?

I went to the Vice President of Flight Operations. He had been keeping tabs on my progress, because we had flown together years before and were friends. He was astounded. There was nothing negative in my training file. He said they had been messing with me and promised I would never have to deal with anything like this again. Sure enough, he replaced one of the worst offenders, the head of 747 training.

**I lied. I do cry sometimes.
But I never give up.**

Copilot at last!

BANGKOK

My eyes are closed. I'm lying on a thin mattress, on a platform in a large room. There's a roof overhead, but the walls are open. There must be fifty people surrounding me, and they are all wearing saffron colored tops and loose, brown shorts. Monks chant as a breeze blows over us. I can't understand a word. Cool air from the fans feels good, but the actual temperature is 110 degrees Fahrenheit with 75% humidity.

The Wat Poh temple in Thailand is famous for having the largest horizontal Buddha in the world—a huge, gold, reclining statue. Its toes are gigantic and it's truly impressive. But I wasn't there for the Buddha. Wat Poh is also famous for its massage school.

For 180 baht I could get a one-hour massage. Usually, I stayed for two or three. Three hours cost me twenty-one American dollars, twenty-five if I included a tip and paid for a clean sheet, as I always did. This time, I came with another pilot, Jon, who likes long massages, too. He says this is the only place in the world where he can find relief from his constant pain. Jon was eating at a Mexican restaurant in the states when a huge ceiling beam fell on his shoulder. He says he was lucky. The beam missed his infant niece, on the floor in her carrier beside him, by inches.

My masseuse is a master at her craft, and she turned me into putty within minutes. Now she is using her feet and knees on my back and shoulders. The masseuses sing songs in their beautiful Thai language and my cares melt away. She turns me over to work on my front, and I glimpse the gold spires and tiled roofs around me. I love coming to Thailand. The language is beautiful, both written and oral. The people

are peaceful and content. They seem truly happy, even though they are
poor and live in a crowded, dirty city.

The smog was the worst part about Bangkok. The air was so thick and brown that we joked about cutting it with a butter knife. Flying in on a visual approach, we never told the controllers we had the "runway in sight" until we were almost landing because we couldn't see it. There wasn't a cloud in the sky, but the visibility was non-existent. I was so glad when our company installed TCAS in our planes—a Terminal Collision Avoidance System that warned of approaching traffic and told us whether to climb or descend to avoid a collision. The controllers were difficult to understand, too, more so than most of Asia. Rarely could we see some of the gorgeous temples and surrounding countryside on final approach.

One time, on a two-day layover, the other two pilots were going to Pat Pong, Bangkok's sex district. I knew it would be shocking, but I wanted to experience it. The lead flight attendant and I stuck to the guys like glue as we walked into the captain's favorite place. There was a sex show on stage, and we sat in a booth where we were immediately joined by two young women. The cocktail waitress brought us Singha beers in glasses that didn't look clean. I hoped the alcohol would kill anything on them. The copilot moved to the inside so I would protect him, but then the prostitute started hitting on me! I finally convinced her I wasn't interested. The captain was.

The bathroom for females was on the other side of the men's. We had to walk through the urinals to get to it. It was so gross that I slowed my drinking down and only used it once. We stayed until four a.m., although I'm not sure why. Mostly, I stayed because they stayed, and I wouldn't go back to the hotel by myself. Besides, we had the next day off. The captain left in a tuk-tuk with two women and we didn't see him the rest of the layover. That was the first and last time I saw Pat Pong.

My favorite activity was the Chao Phraya River tour. Streets were an afterthought, since Bangkok used to be totally accessible by boat. This is one of the main reasons Bangkok has such horrible traffic problems. On the river you could get the feel of the old Thailand, or Siam. Baby cribs rocked in the breeze, and the colorful designs and beautifully shaped roofs gave an odd sense of peace as you drifted by on the filthy, polluted waterway. "Keep your lips tightly shut when another boat goes by," I was told the first time I went.

We stopped at the snake farm whenever there were new pilots or flight attendants with us. There are jumping snakes, cobras, and all sorts of vipers. I'm surprised they don't lose more tourists, because the snake handlers are always shoving the snakes into your face, trying to elicit fear. Never sit down by the arena. You have to fake bravery you don't always feel because the more afraid you seem, the more they try to scare you. I've heard that the farm loses at least three employees a year from snake bites and I believe it.

I love to go sightseeing, and I make my plans as soon as I see my schedule for the month. The captains I fly with joke that it is refreshing to be with someone who enjoys their job as much as I do, and they often go with me. I'll never forget the first time we went to the Jim Thompson house.

Jim Thompson had been a well to do silk merchant, born in my home state of Delaware. He was credited with starting the silk industry in Thailand. A lover of the Thai people and culture, his home was an art lover's haven. It was actually seven Thai houses, turned outside in, because Jim thought the outside walls were the most beautiful.

Elephant riding and temple gazing in Bangkok.

One day, while vacationing in Malaysia, Jim took a walk into the jungle and never returned. No piece of him was ever found. He disappeared without a trace, so they couldn't pronounce him dead. His house in Bangkok was kept ready for his return. Rumor had it that he was with the CIA. The Thai government appropriated his house and turned it into museum nine years later.

Severely crippled beggars were everywhere in Bangkok. Maimed by their family at birth, they were "honored" because they earned enough to feed their entire family. Early each morning they were carried to a spot where there would be plenty of foot traffic and placed on the ground with a bowl to collect money, or baht. It was sad to see.

Bangkok crowds reminded me of Times Square on New Year's Eve. It was hard not to get claustrophobic, and my feet barely touched the ground. Add in humidity and pollution, and some days I practically ran back to my hotel room.

Contrasts.
I love Bangkok. I hate Bangkok.
I wish I had time to see the rest of Thailand...

Tum Nuk Thai was one of my favorite restaurants in Bangkok.

Copilot, Boeing 747.

My 747.

BOMBS

Taking off out of Seattle's Seatac Airport I never guessed what the day would hold. The sky was clear and our freighter roared into it, waking up people below. We turned north and the controller gave us a clearance direct to Anchorage, Alaska. It was early morning and we were alone in the sky.

We leveled at 32,000 feet. I monitored the radios; the captain unplugged and leaned his head back, tired from moving to a new house. The flight engineer was back making coffee and using the lavatory. It was a glorious day to be flying and I took everything in. Victoria, Canada passed below us—we had vacationed there a few years back. I could see the ferry boats moving between Victoria and Vancouver. My kids loved putting Canadian toonies into the massage chairs on those ferries.

"Our reports are that a light twin has just hit one of the twin towers in New York City," Air Traffic Control said.

What? The controller was talking to another pilot on a different frequency.

"No, no other information yet. It was either a twin or an airliner."

Surprised, I looked over at the captain. He was still unplugged. I told him what they were talking about and he just shrugged, uninterested. I kept listening.

Both towers had been hit. The flight engineer came back up front and I relayed the conversation to him. "What have you been smoking while I was gone?" he asked, laughing.

"At first they thought it was a light twin," I said. "Then the report came in that it was an airliner, now they're saying two airliners." Finally, the captain sat up straight in his chair. By now we were all listening to the radio. It was surreal. Air Traffic Control closed the continental United States airspace behind us as we flew north.

More reports came in as we flew on to Anchorage. A Delta Air Lines flight was arriving from Tokyo, landing in Portland, Oregon. Seattle Center informed them that the continental United States was closed and asked them where they wanted to land.

"Portland, Oregon, sir," came the reply. They had not heard.

"Ah, Delta, I repeat, Portland is closed, where would you like to go?"

The Delta pilot did not sound flustered, just tired. He had, after all, been up all night. He repeated that Portland, Oregon was his destination.

"Delta, the whole continental United States is closed. Pick another place to land."

A long silence followed. Finally, the Delta pilot answered "Vancouver." Then, worried that he would be misunderstood, he quickly added "Canada. Vancouver, Canada, Sir." The controller rogered that, then had us switch frequencies. We were laughing, not at the Delta pilot, but probably to release tension concerning the whole situation. *Nothing like this had happened before.*

The sky was a ghost town. We were the only plane on the frequency, talking to the controller. He informed us that both towers had collapsed. We were incredulous. *Maybe they were damaged, but collapsed?*

Landing in Anchorage hours later, we parked, collected our bags, and walked across the ramp. Everyone was so somber. We went inside and were directed upstairs to watch the television coverage. Horrified we watched as the buildings fell, over and over, on replay. It had never occurred to us that airplanes could be used as bombs.

Everyone in the nation was in shock, but we, as pilots, had our paradigm shattered. I called home to inform my husband that I was fine. He told me to call the school to let the kids know. My eyes filled with tears as the kids in my daughter's class cheered when the secretary made the announcement that I was safe.

Shaken, we were driven to our hotel. The flight engineer and I rented a car and drove south to Portage Glacier for the day. Unbeknownst to us, downtown Anchorage was being evacuated. A plane was arriving from Asia without radio communication and authorities feared the worst. My kids were watching, horrified, as the news reported this breaking development. It turned out to be nothing.

Flags flew at half-mast that night as I ate dinner. The waitress and I cried. Next I went to Humpys, a local restaurant and bar in downtown Anchorage. There must have been fifty airline employees filling the outside patio with raucous drinking and conversation. We were all stranded indefinitely. The captain begged off any activity and slept the better part of three days. The engineer was in his room resting, because his back went out on him earlier that day while we were sightseeing. Mine did the same the next morning. Stress does funny things to a body.

Three days later we were deadheaded to Minneapolis, Minnesota; then deadheaded to Los Angeles to continue our trip. We were subdued and wary for the next week in Asia, but nothing else happened. Our trip was uneventful, but we acted like sleepwalkers, numbly getting through each day. Cell phone covers were for sale in Singapore and Hong Kong proclaiming "Bin Laden Hero." We weren't in Kansas anymore.

Things have changed since 9/11. Our security is tighter, but we were already on alert. Many years before there had been a plan to blow up eleven 747s out of Tokyo—The Bojinka Plot. It was thwarted, but we began searching our airplanes routinely, matching bags to passengers and other precautions, way back then. The only thing that altered significantly for us was airport security. It was now a hassle, even for flight crews. Some pilots retired early rather than be subjected to constant scrutiny at security checkpoints. Most of us realized it was a necessary evil. We submitted, grumbling, acknowledging that anyone could get a flight crew uniform and fake identification. The rumor was still rampant that one of the terrorists had been a jumpseating "pilot." This would make all the cockpit door reinforcements a farce if a terrorist was already up front.

Nine eleven was a wake-up call for all of us, but we also realized that even pilots cannot control everything. People asked me if I was afraid to fly, after 9/11. I wasn't. I asked them if they were afraid of tall buildings. They looked at me without comprehending. Being in the twin towers in New York City Tuesday morning, September 11, 2001 killed more people than being in any plane crash ever has.

All you can do is your best.
Control is an illusion.

SAFETY

"Whoa, lady pilot, you are in the wrong place."

No shit Sherlock. I was in the middle of the Tenderloin District, one of San Francisco's worst areas, at 11:30 at night. I had gone to see Phantom of the Opera. When it was over, the streets cleared out and I was alone. There wasn't a cab to be had. I had no choice but to start walking back to my hotel. That is how I ended up two blocks too far to the south, surrounded by drug dealers and junkies, pimps, and prostitutes.

It was dark. I was scared and walking fast. Who in the world knew I was a pilot? A man walked toward me out of the shadows.

It was the beggar I met on the street this afternoon. I had even gave him some yen, something totally out of character for me. Everyone in San Francisco has their hand out. There are three homeless people on each block walking from my hotel to the Financial District. I would go broke if I gave everyone money.

"Spare some coin?"

"I only have yen," I said, not slowing down my pace.

"Whoa. You've just been to Japan? I was there years ago."

I stopped. We talked for half an hour, and he told me about his days in the service in Asia. He said he could get yen exchanged, so I gave him some. Now here he was.

"Let me walk you back to your hotel. Cathedral Hill, right?"

Talk about fate. Or luck, synchronicity, or help from God. It's funny, because I am usually so careful. I call a cab or don't leave my hotel after dark, unlike other women I've met who consider themselves invincible. Once I was flying from Tokyo to Manila as flight engineer on the 747. A lady in business class and I started talking. She was a fashion designer and I complimented her outfit. Even arriving that day from New York she looked fresh and unwrinkled. Her team of designers was headed to their factory in the Philippines.

Scornfully, she mentioned that her boss had wanted to send a man with them for protection. Of course she had refused.

The Philippines is not always the safest place. Three of our male pilots were driven to a warehouse and robbed at gunpoint on the way to their flight. Our company warned us of current safety issues, and we were given rooms on a guarded floor in our hotel. I told her that I would take all the protection I could get.

She already had her mind made up so we agreed to disagree. I hope she was okay. So many career women I have met have chips on their shoulders when it comes to safety. I try not to let my position in a man's world interfere with my good judgment.

One of our female pilots realized she had left her phone card at the train station in Munich, Germany. Instead of getting the other two pilots to go back with her or just forgetting it, she picked up her huge flashlight and headed for the station alone. Three men accosted her and she fought back. The attackers finally ran off, but not before breaking her pelvis.

Another of our pilots accepted a ride from a Korean man who was on his way to his birthday party. "Ever been to a Korean birthday party?" he asked her. Arriving at his apartment she realized, too late, that she was the party. He raped her, but let her go, otherwise unhurt.

Succeeding in this macho career won't keep me safe. I'm not invincible and most people don't care whether I am a pilot.

Life turns on a dime. Like it or not, women are prey. Sometimes even men are prey. Our male pilots have been robbed in Washington D.C., Los Angeles, Amsterdam, and Manila. One was shot in the foot. Others were beaten up.

A bouncer at a Singapore bar told me about the mafia and underground crime in Singapore. He said tourists were safe. Singapore is known as a safe city. You can walk around at any hour and be safe. *But I wouldn't.*

Intuition has served me well. My first lucky escape occurred driving from Florida to California. I stopped to get a room just off the interstate, but the hotels were full. When I got back on the freeway there was a car on my rear bumper. Someone had noticed that I was alone, looking for a hotel.

He sped up and passed me, then turned around on the median strip and headed the other way. *Not for long.* He was soon on my bumper again. My heart was beating fast. He hadn't tried to force me off the road. Yet. Twice more he passed me, turned around, and came up behind me again.

There were no exits for miles, just a rest area ten miles ahead. The next time he passed me I waited until he was on the median. Then I put the accelerator to the floor. I was going over a hundred and slowed down when I reached the rest area exit. There were trucks parked around and I leapt out of the car and ran to the closest one.

A lady trucker opened the door for me and let me in. As I explained my situation, the car that had been following me pulled up down below. Another car pulled up behind it and two men got out. He had been waiting for back up, I suppose. The lady trucker said lone women had been disappearing without a trace. She thought they were transported over the border to Mexico or Central America where white slavery was alive and well. *I was lucky.* I spent the night in the truck and followed her to town the next morning.

My second lucky escape was while I was working as a flight attendant for various rock groups. My day started at three in the morning in Burbank, California. We were flying Elvis Presley's band and singers to Maine and stopped to pick up the other half of the group in Las Vegas, Nevada. En route, over the state of Colorado, Air Traffic Control told the pilots to turn around and return to Las Vegas. Instead, we landed in Colorado Springs and called Graceland. The King was dead. We turned around with a plane full of crying, upset passengers. It was a horrible day.

Around one in the morning, we landed back in Burbank. After putting the airplane to bed, I hopped in my car and headed for home. At a stoplight I noticed a man in an old, beat-up pickup watching me. I was too tired to care. Turning into my apartment complex, I saw him pass me, then hit the brakes. *There was no way it was a coincidence that he was still there, right behind me ten miles down Van Nuys Boulevard.* I drove into my locked garage, parked, and ran for the gate. I had three almost-identical keys for my apartment, gate, and mailbox. Fingering them, I jabbed one in the security gate. The lock turned!

I heard the pickup screech into the driveway. Entering the stairwell, I heard him thud over the wall. Running up as fast as I could, I wondered which key would open my apartment at the top of the stairs. Jabbing the next one in, it also turned and I rushed in. I threw myself onto the floor under the window sill in the dark shadow. The man thundered out of the stairwell and I saw his shadow on the floor beside me. He was looking in my window! I held my breath as he moved off, but I didn't move. Sure enough, he was waiting for me to make a move. He walked back by in the other direction, knowing I had to be close. When I heard his footsteps get further away, I crawled as fast as I could to the bedroom and called the police. He was long gone by the time they got there.

My third close call was in Minnesota. After being divorced for a year I decided it was time to move into the dating arena. I agreed to a dinner date with a pilot I met at work. He picked me up and we went to a restaurant on the Mississippi River. We started with a bottle of wine and an appetizer.

Halfway through, before dinner, I realized he gave me the creeps. *He had dead eyes. Shark eyes.* There was no one in there. It was like looking into two black holes. I pretended I was sick and told him I needed to go home. He got angry, but we left.

Walking me to the door, he tried to kiss me goodnight but I ducked inside and closed the door. He pushed it open before I could lock it. He said he needed to use the bathroom. *Now he was in my house.*

Coming out of the bathroom, he said he wasn't feeling good either and better spend the night on my couch. "Ssh. Keep your voice down. You'll wake the girls," I lied. Perplexed, he said he thought my daughter was at the babysitter's house. She was, I said, but I had them come home at bedtime because Darcie slept better in her own bed.

Did he believe me? Every time he started to talk, I shushed him. I guided him to the door and firmly shoved him out and locked it. He drove away. Then I broke down, crying and shaking.

Later I couldn't believe my behavior was so bizarre. *Was I nuts? My first date and I panicked?* I didn't even make it through dinner.

I would be single for a long time, once word got around. If anyone ever asked me out again...

Riding from the parking lot to the terminal with the flight attendants a few weeks later, I listened to their whispered conversation. There was a pilot who had been date raping them. He would walk them to their rooms on layovers, on the pretense of safety. Always a gentleman, he would look under the bed for them, check the shower, and behind the curtains. Then, alone in the room, he would push her onto the bed and rape her. It was his word against hers and he always won.

Horrified, I pushed for details. A name? They wouldn't tell me who he was and they were terrified. Could you tell me his initials? SH.

I gasped. And said his name. They quickly shut me up, hoping the other male pilots hadn't heard. I wanted to shout it from the rooftops, but I was afraid of him, too. And there was no proof.

You can't control everything...
but you can stay vigilant.

FREIGHTER DAWGS

We level off at 29,000 feet, the highest we can climb our 'whale' (747) when we are this heavy. As we burn off fuel, we will continue to climb up in thousand foot increments. In "the old days," when I was flying on the 747 as a flight engineer, we often climbed too early, just to get the altitude before someone else did. Or, we would get stuck down too low and our fuel burn would be huge. We would be wondering if we could make it to Japan without stopping or declaring a fuel emergency. Now we have radar, and Air Traffic Control can keep an eye on us, so the parameters are tighter and we can be more flexible.

I check the weather in Japan, just to make sure there aren't any surprises. As much as I enjoy the flight attendants, the freedom of being able to walk around and get my own meals whenever I'm hungry is a huge plus. On freighters we can choose our entrees, and the trays are loaded with extras like Snickers bars, cheese and crackers, sandwiches, etc. It is like having a picnic at 37,000 feet. Once, one of our captains was furious that they hadn't loaded meals on his flight. He knew there was fresh salmon downstairs, so he took his pocketknife (obviously pre-9/11!) out and cut a huge slab for lunch. The company nearly fired him—instead they charged him $500 for the salmon he ate.

Being on a freighter is more relaxing than flying passengers, and we don't have to worry about how smooth the ride is because the boxes don't care about turbulence and neither do we. There is something about having a plane as huge as the 747 to yourself.

Freighters are not tied to the same rules as passenger departures, and we could leave when we were loaded. It is like having your own private plane, except that when we look out the cockpit door, we can see all the way back to the tail—230 feet!

We loved our Anchorage cargo base.

Pulling out the manifest from a box in the cockpit, you can read what you have on board each flight. Most of the time we have unidentifiable boxes with generic contents, but you never know until you look. We fly prototypes of new cars that are secret and tightly wrapped to hide their identity. Sometimes we have computers and video games, other times we have clothes. We joke about needing new computers when we have thousands on board. *Who would miss just one?*

I've flown everything from valuable art shipments—the art curator told us the value could not be accurately estimated, but that it was in the billions—to 250,000 pounds of McDonald French fries fried in canola oil—with the Mad Cow Scare going on, Asians would not eat the French fries when they learned they were fried in beef fat. There were ten flights that flew across the Pacific full of French fries that night. Jay Leno was cracking jokes about the bonfire if we went down in flames, but I was more worried about the amount of dry ice it took to keep them frozen—too much dry ice was prohibited because it could freeze our flight controls.

The entire nose of our freighter lifts up for long pallets, and the stairs leading to the cockpit have to be raised until the loading is complete. I love it when we have animals. One night I had hundreds of ferrets, and the next I had thousands of baby chicks. The air and engine noise are loud, so I wear ear plugs, but I could still hear the chicks peeping all the way across the ocean! Sometimes we have salt water fish in thousands of gallons of water. Once we had a whole zoo of antelope, pigs, and zebras, bound for Bangkok. One crazy zebra kicked his way out of his crate. The handler nailed the crate back together with a hammer he brought along just in case.

When planes first began carrying animals there were some deadly crashes. The animals moved towards the tail, changing the center of gravity too much, stalling the plane on takeoff. Now animals are tightly crated in pallets that lock in place. Tonight we have a Brahma bull that must weigh two thousand pounds. He grunts instead of mooing, and he is so long—he must stretch twelve feet, front to back. How does a backbone support something that heavy? Looking down on him, I think I could ride him because he is tightly crated. Maybe on my next walk… Then I remembered the escapee zebra. What if I'm down there stretching my legs and I turn around and see a huge Brahma bull charging me? It would be like the streets of Pamplona with nowhere to run unless you could reach the stairs in time…

There were two beautiful giraffes on board one time. As high as our freighter ceiling is, the adult still had to bend her neck unless she was lying down. But we were carrying them too far—Cleveland through Houston through San Francisco, Anchorage, Tokyo and on to Bangkok. The baby didn't make it. The handler just shook his head and said that sometimes it happens, and that giraffe are like sheep—they don't fight; when they are stressed they just give up and lay down and die. I was so angry. *Why wouldn't you get a more direct flight for them?*

We carry horses and cows, too, and we have to be careful not to exceed the humidity ratio in the plane. Excessive water vapor can't be handled by our systems, and we don't want our cables to ice up at cruise. The horses were draft horses, going to Japan. *To be eaten.* The Japanese cut the horse meat into three inch squares and marinate it before eating it raw. I'm glad I've never flown the horses because I would want to save them all.

Flying pigs around Asia permeates our clothes, even the clothes inside our suitcases. All we have to do is submit our entire wardrobe to laundry with the word "pigs" on our form and they are washed without question *for free*. Now the company gives us trash bags to put our suitcases in whenever we have pigs on board. When I was a flight engineer, it was my job to do the outside walk around and check the cargo compartment to see that all the pallets were locked down securely. Years ago, flying to Anchorage, twelve pigs were loaded near the tail, two hundred feet behind the cockpit, stacked four levels high. They smelled to high heaven. It was a three-hour flight from Seattle to Anchorage, with a long layover. My husband and daughter were waiting for me at the hotel. When I walked into the room to kiss him good morning, his reaction was to hold his nose and say, "You smell like a pig! Go take a shower!"

I've flown all of our freighters, and they are all configured differently. Every freighter we own has different engines, instruments, specifications, and layouts. But we are trained in all the configurations, and it usually isn't a problem. One thing never changes—the uncomfortable cockpit seats. Our airline decided not to invest in the expensive seats for their pilots. I think it would have saved the company money in the long run, because so many of our pilots have back problems. This means that they have to be compensated for their early retirement, or for their surgeries and missed days of work. It gets expensive to pay pilots for not working, and spending an extra $1,500 to get a seat that is ergonomically designed is cheap in comparison.

When Northwest Airlines phased out the passenger 747s, Anchorage was the only 747 base left in our system and it was all freight. Beginning and ending my trips in Alaska, I realized how much more the pilots who were based there knew. It surprised me to learn they used the tide tables to help plan the fuel load! Even though our dispatchers scoffed at first, Alaska pilots knew that tides could foretell whether Anchorage was going to be socked in by fog when the sun came up—meaning you needed to be prepared with extra fuel to go to an alternate airport like Fairbanks—or be clear.

When I checked out as captain, I was thrilled to have Anchorage copilots who knew the ropes. They knew Alaska conditions better than the dispatchers and regular line pilots. Icy runways, crappy conditions, maximum crosswinds, low fog—these were my new normal. Sure, I flew into Alaska before I was captain, but now I was getting a trial by fire.

We flew into Anchorage one morning after flying all night. A United Airlines flight reported wind shear and gusts on the east runways that were over our allowable maximum, a real problem when we were already committed to landing. Now what? Fairbanks was only twenty minutes away, but the huge fuel burn at low altitude closed that door to us. We tried another runway to no avail… I came in high and hot, padding the speed for the turbulence and wind shear, and had to go around. Kenai was not plowed wide enough for a 747, and Elmendorf hadn't had a landing in over an hour—their braking conditions were fair, and we guessed they had wind shear conditions similar to Anchorage International.

Crewmembers are the best resources a captain has. I was a copilot or flight engineer most of my career, and the best captains were the ones who valued my opinion. My engineer wanted to go to Elmendorf, but she was new to Anchorage, like me. My copilot, a seasoned Alaska veteran, suggested landing on runway 6 in

Anchorage, even if there was still wind shear. We had handled conditions there before, he reasoned, and knew the runway. I took his advice. We landed on runway 6 with no problems.

The freighters were retired when the Anchorage base closed, taking a part of Northwest Airlines' history with them. None of us wanted to be regular pilots when we were used to being cool freight dogs. Flying tsunami relief supplies to Asia was incredible… we felt like we were making a difference in people's lives. And flying animals and cargo was so much fun. Regular line flying just couldn't compare.

Freighter pilots are called dogs because they are
"dog tired" from flying all night.

Our dog Bear, on the left.
Right, the nose on our freighter lifts up for loading longer pallets.

FIRED

Pulling up at the terminal of Hong Kong's new airport on Lantau Island, the three of us grudgingly admitted that it was an incredible facility. Built on landfill in the South China Sea, the runways were longer and there was less of a wind shear problem. Unfortunately, the wind shear problems weren't eliminated. They couldn't cut the top off of Lantau Island by three thousand feet as planned because the environmentalists protested and won. But the new airport is safer. Our flight today is a short hop to Osaka, three hours and ten minutes, followed by a fifty-hour layover. We joke about flying from layover to layover, party to party, and we are ready to leave Hong Kong. It was over a hundred degrees and the worst air pollution day on record. The air shimmers in the intense heat.

I miss the old airport in Hong Kong's Kowloon district, even though the sewage smells taxiing in were asphyxiating. The old airport was a challenge, with its short runway—water on one end and mountains on the other, severe crosswinds, bad weather, and wind shear. I loved the approach and its turn at the checkerboard. I loved flying between the massive hills with buildings towering all around. You could practically see inside the apartments on final. On days with no weather issues, the more focused the pilot flying seemed on approach, the more ribbing we gave him. "Wow, look in that apartment. Is she naked? Oh my God, she is!" We would all end up laughing, with the pilot relaxing and taking a breath. The guys tried it on me, too, but I told them it wouldn't work unless they said, "There's a hot, naked guy!"

Clark, the captain, pointed to a 747 freighter on the ramp as our limousine pulled up to the terminal. "Hey, we get the new one, 6743. They must have finished it." The flight engineer and I didn't have a clue what he was talking about and said so. "The one that was down here three months for modification. Now all our freighters are alike." We nodded. Several of our freighters had been acquired from other airlines and they had significant differences from the ones we already had. Anchorage pilots usually flew the freighters, so they received special training and a book on the unmodified airplanes. Clark, an Anchorage-based pilot, said the company told him to throw his book away last month because the final freighter, 6743, was almost done. The flight engineer and I were Minneapolis-based, but now we understood. Sweating, we carried our bags into the terminal.

Inside, a group of guys were waiting for us. Four of the men were from our airline's Technical Operations department in Minneapolis, and they'd be flying along with us. They'd overseen the changes on the plane, and had been here the whole time.

"So, how's it look? The airplane's generic now?" Clark asked them. He's jovial and well liked, an easygoing guy who is great to fly with.

The techs all looked at each other and exchanged glances. Laughing uncomfortably, one of them finally said, "Not even close. After three months of working on it, we finally gave up. We couldn't get rid of that third autopilot after all. All the CADCs are looking for it, working or not, it has to be installed. The instrument transfer system is different, too, but we'll show you how to use that once we're in the air."

Now it was our turn to exchange glances. "We're just lucky to be getting out of here," one of them continued, and the others agreed.

"We had flames coming out of the instrument panel a week ago."

"We were supposed to have another test flight, but we didn't have time," another man informed us.

"Yeah, they've been trying to schedule revenue freight on this for the last two weeks. That's the earliest window we gave them. If we don't get it out of here today, we lose our bonus."

We looked at each other in disbelief. Caring about their bonus is the last reason in the world to take an airplane.

We arrived at the airplane, and as the men stowed their belongings below, Clark told us that if we felt uncomfortable about any of this we could shut it down. We decided to do our preflights before making any decision one way or the other.

The flight engineer's panel had very few differences and most of the changes were complete, so Les went outside to preflight. The cockpit was hot and crowded. One of the guys from Technical Operations was behind me, watching, and two men from Hong Kong Operations were behind him to "hurry us along." I started preflighting my side of the instrument panel. The radio altimeter didn't preflight the way it normally did—this one only went to 100 feet, then spun a couple of times. I showed Clark.

"Oh, that's because we had to install a DC9 altimeter. We couldn't get the 747 one to work," Mr. Tech Ops interrupted. "I'll explain the rest of the differences in the air."

My eyes widened in shock, as did the captain's.

"We'll try to get you an EP-19 on it by Anchorage. No one is up yet in Minneapolis with the authority to sign it off," he continued.

"Anchorage? We're just going to Osaka. And we need it before takeoff," Clark said, preflighting his side.

"We just need you to limp it to Osaka for us, then." The man was exasperated with our thoroughness.

I was "in-the-books" trying to locate information on the different systems and changes. The captain was talking to the tech who was explaining how the instrument transfer system worked and what they had done, since Clark had said after takeoff would not work for him. I couldn't find the pages, so I listened in.

Things were getting worse and worse. The flight deck was like an oven. A greenhouse. Even with the ground air conditioning we were being roasted alive. The cell phones and ACARs kept ringing. Dispatch, engineering, and flight planning were telling us to "get out of town." Two hours went by while we waited for paperwork. The last thing we needed was pressure when we already had doubts about the airworthiness of the plane. Pilots work through things methodically, and when too many people are giving us advice, we shut down.

Another hour later, dripping with sweat, Clark, Les, and I traipsed into flight operations to call Minneapolis about our concerns. The head of 747 training in Minneapolis thought *we* were being unreasonable. "The training on the differences is no big deal—just a formality," he said. *Not to us.* Combined with the flames, the DC9 altimeter, the missing EP-19, and not understanding the systems that were different, we were uneasy. *We weren't test pilots and we didn't want the FAA to violate us, either.* Frustrated and tired, we finally refused the airplane for "safety" reasons, an unarguable point.

The Technical Operations guys were furious, especially the head boss, who had hardly spoken to us. We apologized, grabbed our bags, and left. We showered and changed back at the hotel and met in the Clark's room for new orders from crew scheduling and a well-deserved beer. A bellhop hand-delivered our messages from crew scheduling that said we were now taking another freighter out the next afternoon. Hallelujah. None of us had refused an airplane before, and we were worried about repercussions. Now it appeared we were back to business as usual.

Hong Kong was still too hot as we walked down Jaffe Road, looking for a good place to eat dinner. Hong Kong comes alive at night and is a great place to be, even with the smog and heat. I slept in the next morning, tired from our ordeal. As I was getting packed and ready to go, my phone rang. It was our dispatcher in Japan, saying the freighter was canceled. He didn't know what we were going to fly next. I called the captain, and we all met in his room. Déjà vu.

Clark had been trying to return calls to Minneapolis, but no one answered. Late the night before, when he returned to his room, there had been a message to call the Vice President of Flight Operations, Jeff Carlson. He hadn't called then, deciding that, having had a few beers, he should wait until morning. Of course, morning in Hong Kong is night in Minneapolis and no one was in.

I decided to call Minneapolis crew scheduling, since the Japanese crew schedulers didn't know anything. My friend Sue answered. "Kathy! Where have you been? You were supposed to be on flight 17 from Hong Kong to Narita this morning!"

"Hong Kong to Narita? They told us we were flying a freighter this afternoon."

"No. You were deadheading to Narita, then Seattle, then Minneapolis for a hearing on Tuesday with Vice President Carlson, the lawyers, and stenographers. They want to fire you!"

"What?" I repeated it back to Sue, so that the other two crewmembers could hear me. *Unbelievable.* Sue put me on hold and came back with a new plan. We would deadhead on tomorrow's flight to Japan, spend the night in Narita, then deadhead on to Minneapolis. We would skip Seattle and a meeting with the Seattle chief pilot, who wasn't returning our phone calls either. I hung up, and faced the guys in disbelief. What had happened? How had this gone so wrong? Perplexed, we reviewed yesterday's actions. This was crazy. We had done the right thing. It must be a mistake. The captain called the union, but no one was there to return our phone call, so he left a message. Going out later, we were afraid this might be our last layover in Hong Kong ever.

Arriving in Narita the next day, we took the bus to the hotel. It isn't legal for the company to deadhead us straight back to Minneapolis without a break according to our contract, so a stop in Japan was required. I went over to Narita crew scheduling to get more documentation of our assignment the day before. We needed hard-copy evidence of our decision. I also talked to a friend in engineering there to see what had happened to our airplane.

The engineer said another crew was brought in to fly it out of Hong Kong, an Anchorage crew with the differences training. There were no mechanical difficulties, and it was now in Minneapolis. So we could have flown it to Osaka without consequences... I asked about the EP-19s. There were still two outstanding. The one on the altimeter was filed. He said EP-19s didn't have to be on the airplane, but they do have to be on file. Plus, there was a safety equipment issue that needed to be fixed. I was surprised. Our company usually does a good job with maintenance.

Back at the hotel lobby, I ran into a union representative. He was looking for us and the hotel told him we had not checked in. He said they were calling us the "Stealth Crew" since we were never in our rooms and we never returned phone calls. They thought we were avoiding them! We asked him why they had a hearing set up. Apparently the head of Technical Operations told Minneapolis we had turned the aircraft down to go drinking in Hong Kong. *Quite an accusation.* We knew he was angry, but we didn't expect him to lie. The $25,000 bonus must have been quite a motivator.

The ALPA representative was surprised to hear our side of the story. He tried to call Minneapolis to straighten things out, but no one would answer his phone calls either. Sometimes, with the time difference on the other side of the world, confusion reigns. You might as well be on two different planets.

Unable to sleep, I finally called Seattle check-in at midnight because it was morning in Seattle, and Ruthie put me through to the chief pilot at his home, on a three-way call, because he was avoiding us, too. The chief pilot didn't sound happy to hear from me. I told him what really happened. He was surprised, and warmed up almost immediately, because he had been told the "drinking in Hong Kong" story. He said not to worry about the hearing, because he would handle it, and that it sounded like a big misunderstanding. *I'll say.*

We arrived in Minneapolis the next day. The hearing was canceled, thanks to the Seattle Chief Pilot, but the meeting was still happening the next day at two p.m. The ALPA representatives would accompany us, and the company would not have lawyers or stenographers present. *What a relief.*

We look happy, but we're faking it.

Looking out at the Hong Kong skyline the next afternoon,
I wondered how things had gone so wrong.

I went out to dinner with a girlfriend to the Mall of America. My children's birthdays were the next week, so it was a good chance to shop for them. I wasn't worried anymore because I knew we did the right thing. I hadn't ever been as worried as the guys, but I was angry, and I ranted. I couldn't comprehend how we could be in trouble for doing the right thing. I would go to the newspapers if I had to. The press would have a field day with a crew in trouble for refusing an airplane for safety issues. My girlfriend is a lawyer and she agreed there was no way they could legally discipline us for doing the right thing. My husband wasn't as convinced, and said as much when I called home.

The next day at the hearing, the Vice President of Flight Operations stormed into the room. As we shook hands, I reminded Mr. Carlson I had worked in training while I was pregnant, and that I had made him a manual. A little taken aback, Jeff thanked me, then got right to the point. "Why did you turn down a perfectly good airplane?"

Five days before we had faxed in our Air Safety Reports. The captain was shocked to learn Vice President Carlson hadn't seen them. If he hadn't read our reports, who had he been talking to? So Clark read our report, word for word.

I watched the Vice President's expression. He didn't appear to be listening. His face was livid, and he was getting angrier by the minute. When Clark finished, Vice President Carlson informed us the airplane had been flying around for a week now with no problems *whatsoever.* He couldn't believe a crew with our experience and good reputations had turned it down.

Clark said that it was his decision and that if there were any time off as punishment, he would take it personally, instead of us.

Our captain was a stand-up guy, but *time off*? We hadn't done anything wrong!

Vice President Carlson piled his papers as if he were done with us and was leaving. Almost as an aside, he asked if I had anything to add, and seemed surprised that I did. I don't think he wanted to listen to me, either.

I never broke eye contact with him as I told him about the 120-degree day, the worst air pollution on record, and the long layover in Osaka. I stressed that we had every reason to *go* to Osaka, not *stay* in Hong Kong. I told him about the flames behind the instrument panel and that they should have taken another test flight but didn't have time. I told him about the bonus, the revenue freight, the phone calls, the impatience of everyone hurrying us, and the EP19s. None of this was well-documented in the Air Safety Report. I swear his face relaxed as realization dawned. Les added a few more details. Vice President Carlson asked us to leave the room while he made his decision.

When we were called back in, we received a full apology and first class tickets home. Vice President Carlson promised nothing negative would go into our files, and he made us promise to call him personally, at home, if anything like this happened again. Then he admonished us again for turning down a "perfectly good airplane."

I got mad. Teeth gritted, I told him his "perfectly good airplane" was still illegal with two outstanding EP-19s and a safety equipment issue. The ALPA representative kicked me under the table, warning me not to say anything else, but I was tired of being second-guessed.

Vice President Carlson asked the man in the room from manuals and revisions if this was true. The man nodded. This time

President Carlson apologized without an admonition and gave us first class tickets home.

He reiterated that there would be no retaliation and that we could check all three of our files at any time. He did add that we couldn't get in trouble for the EP-19s, that the company would.

Afterwards the ALPA representative said he had never seen Vice President Carlson change his mind about anything, ever, and that he was shocked. Clark and Les kept slapping me on the back, saying, "Good job." They were just happy we hadn't been fired. I was still angry. Who would believe a flight crew would turn an airplane down to go drinking? We weren't even given the professional benefit of the doubt.

Later I asked a friend of mine with the FAA if we could have been violated for taking the airplane if they had caught the open EP-19s. He said, "Of course. We can't get to the company so we violate the pilots." Bingo.

Make the right decision and go for it.

I love Hong Kong, but I would never risk my job to stay there.

South China Sea.

A JAL flight above us in a holding pattern.

BUNKROOMS

I hate sitting in coach. Being an airline pilot has ruined it for me. Our union negotiated for first class deadheading, so now I'm a first class kind of person. Actually, I'm even more spoiled than first class. I'm used to my own my private bunkroom, stretching completely out on a flight.

On our 747s, upstairs just opposite the galley, there was a locked door with a peephole. Inside there were two bunk beds and a narrow aisle to stand up in. The airplane fuselage curves over the top bed, giving you less space up there. The guys always wanted the lower bunk, because it was roomier. Most of the guys are bigger than I am, and it really didn't matter to me, so I always took the top bunk.

Some of the guys wouldn't even come in while I was sleeping, even though I brought pajamas or a long shirt. If you slept in your uniform, it never unwrinkled, and I hated looking like a slob. But their actions probably had less to do with what I sleep in and more with what they slept in: their skivvies. If there was a first class seat, they took it. So, I was used to being in my own private sleeping quarters, like royalty. Lots of pilots have trouble sleeping in the bunks. Not me. I especially love it if it is bumpy, like a rocking chair.

One time I was so dead to the world that I didn't wake up until we were at the gate in Korea. The guys had to knock on the door. I dressed as fast as I could, then raced for customs. Halfway there the copilot realized he had forgotten something on the airplane. Getting back to the airplane in Seoul's old Incheon airport was a maze and he was new, so I offered to go with him.

I love first class.

*Our bunkrooms didn't look as good as these Boeing 787 bunks,
but they were a little more private.*

They had the escalators switched and going the opposite way by the time we returned, and we had to run up them. Mind you, I was in a dead sleep less than fifteen minutes earlier. My blood pressure is low to begin with, but when I'm asleep it drops even lower. As we reached customs, I broke into a cold sweat and almost passed out. I had to sit down and put my head between my knees. Luckily this was years before the bird flu scare, or I could have been quarantined for weeks.

Yes, the bunkroom is my favorite place in the airplane. Once, while sleeping the sleep of the dead, I had the most bizarre dream. The captain was in the room with me, pacing back and forth, growling. I could barely see him in the dark. He looked like a mad man. Why was he growling? How could anyone be that angry? Was it something I did, or something that happened at home before the trip? He seemed like a nice enough guy earlier. I began plotting how to get out of the bunkroom without getting killed. I didn't have my clothes on, and I didn't want to go out into first class in my nightshirt. Just then he leaned over and bit me in the stomach.

Screaming, I sat bolt upright hitting my head on the ceiling. Then I fell out of bed. No, I didn't fall into the galley in my skivvies like one of our pilots did. But I was embarrassed to realize that there was no one pacing in the room. It was dead quiet, and there was a pilot sleeping in the lower bunk beside me, behind the curtain. His clothes were hanging on the hook. Or, maybe he was pretending to sleep, because who can sleep when someone has just screamed, clunked, and clattered to the floor?

Sheepishly, I dressed and went out into the galley. The flight attendant was sitting on her fold-down seat, reading a magazine.

I shook my head, trying to raise my blood pressure and wake up.

"Tough time sleeping?" she asked.

"I was sleeping really well, I think. Dreaming. Then it turned into a nightmare and I fell out of bed."

"Did the guy wake you up with his snoring?" she asked, pointing toward the door where I could now hear the rhythmic shudder that sounded like a growl. You could hear him over the engine and air noise! "He was really loud a little while ago. I'll bet that is what woke you up."

I started laughing, and told her about my dream. Just then the guy did a Snort-snort-snort in his sleep, and I realized that was what happened when he "bit" me. It was almost time for my shift anyway, so I went into the cockpit laughing. The guys had a good chuckle, too, when I told them the story, and the captain assured me he would never bite me.

When it was time for the next shift change, the snorer came into the cockpit. He complained that I woke him up when I fell out of bed, and what was up with that? Laughing, I told him the story, but he was not as amused as the rest of the crew. I asked him if he knew he snored, and he said yeah, his wife complained all the time. I told him I agreed with his wife, and so did the flight attendant—neither of us had ever heard someone snore so loudly. He was still angry, and said I should have worn earplugs. Later, thinking about it, I wondered why you would go into a bunkroom where someone was already asleep if you knew you snored like that.

It's funny how many times I didn't react when the guys were being openly rude. It would have been easy to get churlish and start a fight. But when I was a flight engineer on the 727 I flew with captains and copilots that didn't get along. It was horribly unsafe, and always made me nervous. One nightmarish situation started out with the two guys up front talking about ALPA, our airline pilot union. I can't even remember the details, just that it escalated as the day went on. We were flying the mountain stations, hopping through Billings, Butte, Helena, and Bozeman, Montana. The copilot wouldn't read the checklists and he wouldn't put the gear or flaps down for the captain. I watched the captain retaliate on the next leg. By the time we reached Seattle that evening they were screaming at each other, and nothing I said or did helped.

I decided I would never let that happen with me. I knew you shouldn't discuss politics or religion, and I mentally added union issues to that list. As the years went on, I added women's rights. In the early days with the airline, there were quite a few comments about women not belonging in a cockpit. The topic of how women should be "barefoot and pregnant, at home in the kitchen" came up frequently, and I laughed lightly. Obviously, I was here, so it really didn't matter what they thought.

Unfortunately, they couldn't leave it at that. Sometimes one of the pilots was so overt about his feelings that it was hard not to get defensive or mad. But I remembered that dangerous flight through the mountains, and kept my cool. "You know you're taking that job from a man who needs it to feed his family," a copilot announced one day.

"Yes, that's what my ex-husband used to say, that I got his job. But he never finished college, and Northwest requires college, so how could I take his job?" That seemed to deflate the rising tension, and we started talking about marriage problems instead.

"Northwest only hired military pilots for years, as it should be. Men who have fought defending their country deserve the job," guys would say. I think they were baiting me, or looking for an argument to liven up a dull flight at cruise.

"They're still hiring military pilots, when they can find them," I said. "But the service isn't training as many pilots, so they have to hire from general aviation."

"They don't have to. There are still qualified men with a military background out there who can't get a job. You women are taking them away."

"I doubt that the few women that have been hired have taken that many jobs from them," I say, without emotion.

"Well, what makes you think you deserve to have their job?"

I know, I shouldn't even answer. But I do. "One, I'm qualified. Two, my dad died when I was a little girl, and his death was service connected. Three, my stepdad died when I was eighteen, with complications from the polio he contracted in the Korean War. So I think I've paid my dues, losing two dads, don't you?"

"But what would make a woman want this job? Why didn't you just become a flight attendant?"

"My mom always told me that the best way to be a good mom was to be able to support your family if something happened to your husband. My dad died when I was eight, and Mom couldn't earn enough to feed my brother and me without going back to school."

None of my logic ever made one iota of difference or changed anyone's mind. But at least I didn't have fistfights and knockdown drag-outs in the cockpit. The few times I did lose my cool, when the comments were too rude to ignore, I regretted rising to the bait.

Sometimes the guys were just inappropriate. One captain was giving me directions to a certain shopping area in Bangkok, and described walking through a fish market on the way. "It smells really bad," he said. "Dead fish everywhere, makes you want to hold your nose. Oh, but you're a girl, so it won't bother you. Girls are used to smelling like fish, aren't you?"

Okay, really? What can you say to that? Most of us knew that we were entering a career field where there would be a certain amount of chauvinism and sexism. All the cockpits had lewd comments written in grease pencil about unpopular pilots. Before females and blacks came along, the prejudice was usually directed at "Scabs," fellow pilots who crossed the picket line during a strike or labor dispute. Northwest Airlines was nicknamed "Cobra Airlines" because they were always on strike, and the pilots had long memories. Now they had another target. I knew that the easiest way to handle sexist comments was to ignore them.

Chips turn into rocks that are too heavy to carry day in and day out.

Being pilots for Northwest Airlines is just too much fun!

DEAD BODIES

I knew this title would grab you. It sure grabbed my friend Daryl, who used to haul corpses around in the back of a twin-engine Piper. He absolutely hated his job. Daryl didn't hate the flying or the money. He hated getting up to altitude and having the bodies groan and moan and release gases.

That's what bodies do, he told us. When a human being dies, the muscles relax and all sorts of fluids and gases are released. All the body bags were zipped and sealed, but on a dark night, flying alone, he always got the willies. *What if one of the bodies wasn't really dead? What if they were moaning in pain? What if they were ghosts?*

One night his buddies decided to play a trick on him. They knew how much he hated flying alone with the bodies. One of them, Ray, volunteered to be the "body" and was zipped into a fresh, new body bag. Ray was loaded into the airplane on top of the rest of the corpses, with his head right behind the pilot seat. Unaware, Daryl took off into the starry night.

At altitude Ray began his show. It started as a few discreet moans. Then he let loose some gas. Then he slowly unzipped the bag. The sound was loud, but Daryl tried to ignore it. Rrriiipp. Daryl concentrated on the flying.

Ray moaned. Another fart. He snaked an arm out of the bag. Then he tapped Daryl on the shoulder.

Daryl screamed like a girl. He jumped and hit his head on the roof. But there was no way out of the cockpit; there was no place to

run. Then he heard Ray laughing. Daryl said Ray was laughing so
hard he never felt the pummeling he gave him until later.

WE FLEW INTO Manila through Tokyo, and often we had older, very
ill Filipinos onboard flying back to their native country because it
was their final resting place. The Philippines are incredibly beautiful islands, full of greenery, chocolate hills, mountains, and waterfalls. They wanted to be buried on their home soil. Sometimes they
waited too long.

One Filipino family did not want to get off the plane in Tokyo.
The old man was still asleep by the window, and the others were
just sitting there. "I'm sorry, but you'll have to get off the airplane
now," a flight attendant informed them.

"But we're going on to Manila. Doesn't this plane go on to
Manila?"

"Usually, but not for a few hours. And you still have to get off
and clear Japanese customs and then get back on," she told them
politely.

"I will clear customs for everyone," a young Filipino woman
said. "Give me your passports," she said to the rest of her family.

"No, that won't work. You all need to talk to the customs agents
in person." The flight attendant was tired after a long day.

"But grandpa is asleep and we don't want to wake him. He isn't
feeling well."

"Does he need a doctor?" the flight attendant asked.

"No, no, but he is very tired. This is a long flight for an old man."

"I'm sorry but he has to get off, too."

The family began chattering rapidly in their native language. Finally, one of them told the flight attendant that grandpa could not walk, and she agreed to get him an aisle chair.

Didn't this always happen at the end of the longest day? All she wanted was to go to the hotel and crash onto her bed. Instead she was stuck babysitting this family of stragglers. Tapping her foot impatiently, she glanced over as the family loaded grandpa onto the aisle chair. The man must be exhausted. The blanket slipped off of him and the family hastily put it back. An arm flopped down, and the granddaughter tried to put it across his chest, but it wouldn't bend. The granddaughter tried again. *Rigor mortis!* "That man is dead!" the flight attendant exclaimed.

"No, no, he is just sleeping soundly."

"Then wake him up. I want to talk to him." *She knew he was dead. His limbs were frozen in position.* Of course they couldn't wake him, and the gate agent called a doctor. There was paperwork to be filled out, which Japan is notorious for. It was going to be a much longer day, no doubt about it.

Apparently grandpa expired halfway across the Pacific. The family had decided to "pretend" he was sleeping until they arrived in the Philippines so they wouldn't have to purchase a casket and pay to have him sent the rest of the way in the cargo hold. It was a good plan, in theory. The poor old man had just waited too long to go home.

It was good to be leaving Bangkok, Thailand. The summer heat and smells were powerful enough to knock me out. After two days in a city with heavy traffic, honking horns, dense crowds, and smog so thick you could cut it with a dull knife, I was ready to fly to Japan. Besides, I had spent enough money. Bangkok has great shopping. We were taxiing out for takeoff when Anne, our lead flight attendant, came bursting through the cockpit door in a rage.

"I can't believe they boarded him! I told them no, that he was drunk or stoned or something, and I wouldn't let him on. The agents boarded him though the coach boarding door and told them I had okayed it!"

"No problem. We'll go back to the gate and have them take him off," the captain said. I reached for the radio to talk to flight operations, while the copilot picked up his microphone to call ground control.

"No, no. It's okay. I just want them to know it's unacceptable, what they did. Can you tell flight operations that? He's sleeping now. He said he just had a hard night and he's tired. He won't be any problem."

"Anne, what do you want us to do?" The captain asked her. "It's your call."

"Well, I guess nothing. He was obnoxious and causing problems in the boarding area. Acting strange. They just wanted to board him and be rid of him, but I said no. It just irritates me that they went behind my back and told the south girls I said it was okay. But he's a nice enough guy and he just wants to go home. He came from Nepal."

In the end, we continued and took off. An hour later, Anne came up to see if we needed anything. We asked her about our friend. "He's sleeping. But oh, he looks terrible. If he weren't snoring so loudly I'd think he was dead. He's all waxy and yellow."

I decided to take a walk, just to check him out. I could hear the man's snores from a cabin away, over the engines and wind noise. Thank goodness no other passengers were anywhere near him! And he did look dead. I stopped and stared in fascination. His skin had that surreal stretched look, like a statue in a wax museum. He might have been nice looking if his face weren't so pale. There was absolutely no color to him. When I reported back to the captain and copilot, they both had to go down and look. We entertained ourselves in this manner for an hour or so. Hey, it was a slow day, and obviously pre-9/11.

Three hours later, Anne came bursting in. "He's dead! You guys, he's dead! Oh, I knew I shouldn't have let him on." He was probably just breathing shallowly. Poor Anne was inconsolable. We calmed her down and asked for a doctor on the public address system.

The doctor pronounced the man dead. We contacted Tokyo operations. They asked us to declare the time of death outside the Sea of Japan, so he would die in international waters. We didn't know exactly when he died, so that was no problem. I told operations we would need new seat cushion for 33C.

We covered him with a blanket so the rest of the passengers would think he was sleeping. Anne said he was a businessman, bound for New York, and he definitely looked the part in his suit. His briefcase was up above, in the overhead, and I had to open it to identify him for the Japanese officials.

It was empty. Except for a passport and a necklace, it was empty. No papers, no business cards, no pens. Nothing. Not even a wallet. How weird. Now we were speculating. What was his story? If he wasn't a businessman, who was he? I never forgot his name—Kevin, like my husband.

The captain thought he was smuggling drugs. "He probably swallowed balloons full of cocaine. One of them had a hole and it burst. Overdose."

Well, that would fit the behavior. I kept seeing him in my mind's eye—pale and waxy. I had never seen a freshly-dead man before. We never found out what his story really was.

Life is strange.

Sometimes we look dead after an international flight.

RATS

My friend Cathy came with me on my last trip to Bangkok and I gave her the grand tour of "The City of Angels," as it is also known. We took the river taxi, but didn't stop at the snake farm. She can't stand snakes. For dinner we went to Tum Nuk Thai, an incredible outdoor restaurant that seated 3000 people. The waiters wore roller skates, and all through dinner there was a background hum of wheels going clackety-clack on the boardwalk. We were seated under the moon, up on stilts, on a deck over a garden and creek.

The menu was fifty pages long and Cathy couldn't decide what to eat. She knew she didn't want shark fin soup, or shrimp egg rolls that included the shrimp head. Pad Prick King or Gai Pad Gra Pow? We finally decided on lemongrass chicken and Thai barbecue spareribs. Dinner was delicious. Coconut Lime Pie for dessert topped off the evening, and the temperature was perfect.

"Oh, look! There are cats running around down by the creek," Cathy said.

I looked down and saw them—two-foot long rats beneath us. From a distance they did look like cats. "Well, they do rhyme with cat," I answered, smiling evilly.

Cathy's face lost all color. "They're not cats?"

I shook my head. Thank goodness we had already eaten. I'm pretty sure I had chicken and beef.

SITTING ON THE wall on Sentosa, a popular tourist island in Singapore, Bill Fuchs and I were talking, watching the sun go down over the South China Sea. It had been quite a day. Bill's father was in a Russian prison during World War II, so as we toured the Changi prison, he recounted incredible stories about his dad's life in prison. Then we toured the rest of the island and I almost ended up in a Singapore hospital.

"Here, let me get you and the monkey in the picture," Bill, had said. There were monkeys in the bushes near the Sentosa monorail, and I was taking pictures of them.

"No, I just want a picture of the monkey." *You've heard about the idiots in the United States who provoke the moose and buffalo, then get trampled? That wasn't going to be me.*

"Oh c'mon. It will be a better picture if you're in it." He wouldn't take no for an answer. "Just get a little closer," he said. One step closer… the monkey leapt at me, shrieking! She had babies in the bushes and I was too close. I ran for my life.

I was still shaken, hours later. *Do you know what diseases monkeys carry?* Neither do I, and I didn't want to find out. It reminded me of the guy on the Star Ferry in Hong Kong who tried to commit suicide. The man jumped in the water, knowing he couldn't swim and would drown. Coughing and spluttering, he was saved by some well-meaning bystanders and taken to the hospital. He died ten days later from all the bacteria and pollutants he had swallowed in the Hong Kong Harbor.

So, watching the sun go down, I was finally relaxing. I knew there were salt-water crocodiles nearby, and I would not put one toe in the water. I was safe on my wall. *Then the wall began to move.* It was if it were alive!

Hundreds of rats came out of their holes and began searching for food! Still in prime form after the day's excitement, I leapt off the wall, dragging Bill with me. What a day.

Life is always interesting.

Singapore.

Flight attendants are the best part about flying passengers.

I love talking to kids like this group at Raytheon in Tucson, AZ.

EMERGENCY!

Flying freight is so much easier than flying people, but it isn't as exciting or interesting. I remember my early days on the "three-holer," our nickname for the Boeing 727. None of the passengers had ever seen female pilots before. Everyone would stop at the cockpit door and gawk. I would smile, answer questions, and do my job. It was fun, but my experiences flying rock groups kept me from letting the 'pseudo' fame and notoriety go to my head.

Most of the time when I walked through the cabin passengers didn't realize I was a pilot... they thought I was the head flight attendant. One day we were on final approach to landing when we encountered a problem. The copilot placed the gear handle to the down position and we didn't get the necessary lights to indicate the left main gear was down and locked. It was my job to go check the alignment stripes through the port hole windows in the floor of the cabin.

The captain made an announcement and told the passengers that I would be coming back and not to be alarmed. "Miss, Miss, could I have a scotch and water?" Here we were, circling, trying to land with an emergency, and no fewer than seventeen people asked me for a drink! Apparently they didn't listen to the captain.

Even when I told them I was a pilot they kept asking for drinks. I finally had to ignore them and do my job. On my hands and knees I pulled up the carpet in the appropriate location. The window port was too dirty to see the alignment stripes. Our landing was uneventful and safe, but I've never forgotten that day and the tension I felt on landing hoping the gear was down and locked.

The company organized a publicity flight on the DC10 with three female pilots. The landing in Osaka was greeted with fanfare and a spot on the evening news. Unfortunately, the Japanese did not view the flight in a positive light. The publicity backfired and our bookings dropped for a while after the flight. Asia was still not ready for female pilots or equality.

Another time a lady was complaining that the air conditioner system was leaking alcohol on her. She worried that something was wrong with the airplane, and was getting hysterical. We don't have freon or any other chemicals in our system, so we knew it couldn't be that. The man next to her traded seats with her. He held a cup under the leak and was drinking it! It was hard not to laugh. The captain told me the three overhead luggage bins were connected, and to search the whole module. I checked the bins above and in front of her. There was a bottle of scotch in the overhead that was leaking out and draining backwards!

A flight attendant came up to tell us that a group of Japanese scuba divers was having problems and two of them were writhing in the aisle. Apparently they misread their diving charts and now, up at altitude, were having symptoms of the bends. Our maximum takeoff weight is 833,000 pounds on some of our 747s. Our maximum landing weight is 630,000 pounds. We only burn 25,000 pounds an hour, so if we have to land in the first eight hours of flight, we could be too heavy. We dumped fuel down to landing weight and descended into Seattle. Fuel vaporizes, but it is sad to see that much money come out the nozzles of the wings.

Chicago to Narita was my favorite flight. I was friends with most of the flight attendants and we always had a good time. "There's a drunk in business class complaining of a vibration under his seat." My girlfriend Ellen rolled her eyes, as if to say, "Please, please come placate him." As flight engineer on the 747, it was my job to handle the situation so I went downstairs. I recognized the man because I sat by him on the flight from Minneapolis to Chicago. He had had a couple drinks on that leg, too. "Boy, am I glad to see you," he slurred.

I smiled, but just standing in the aisle I could feel an unusual vibration. He was drunk, but he was right. "Is anyone sitting next to you, by the window?"

"Just you, darlin'," he said, moving over to let me in. I raised the shade, looked out his window, and saw the number two engine.

"Do you know what it is?"

"I think so. I'll be right back." I returned to the cockpit and told the captain the vibration was real—probably the number two engine. The captain pulled the throttle towards idle thrust and I went back downstairs.

"Pretty drunk, isn't he?" Ellen asked. I told her that, drunk as he was, he was also right.

"You're a genius. It stopped," he slurred when I went back to his seat. I agreed, it had stopped. But, I warned him, it might come back and I told him not to worry about it. I didn't tell him we wanted to use the engine en route to Japan as long as we could. Maintenance took the plane out of service for an engine change as soon as we arrived. Passengers and flight attendants can be invaluable resources if you trust them.

Portland Control Tower

PASSENGERS ARE ALWAYS getting sick, especially on long flights, like the Filipinos headed to Manila. I diverted into Anchorage, Alaska twice in a two-week period with passengers having heart attacks. The air traffic controllers in Alaska are friendly and this one recognized my voice. "Weren't you just here last week?" he queried. I laughed and said I was. "Come again next week. It's my birthday and there's a party," he said. I wished him happy birthday but told him I didn't plan to be back…

People. You've got to love them.

EN ROUTE

Flying is hours and hours of boredom broken up by moments of sheer panic.

"I would hate your job. It seems so boring," a passenger told me.

Boring? The first time I heard this comment I thought the man was joking. Women always told me they could never do my job because it was too scary. But boring? I was under the misguided impression that any man who was alive and breathing secretly wanted to fly. Now, over the years, I've heard this opinion expressed many times. Pilots in the service tell me they would never want to fly an airliner—that it is too much like driving a bus. Others mention the unending hotel rooms, the travel away from home, time zone changes, and hours and hours of just sitting up there waiting to land.

Yes, sometimes it may seem boring just cruising along at FL 370 all day. Most of the time boredom is the last feeling I experience after takeoff and climb out. Remember that nothing stays the same, ever. That includes the weather at the destination and en route, the mechanical workings of the plane, and last, but not least, the passengers.

We constantly monitor the instruments, even if it is just a glance every five minutes. Sure, we would get a loud bell for fires, but most of the other problems don't come with an aural warning. The navigation and the radio have to be monitored, too. Between talking to ATC and making position reports to our company, we verify that we're on course and that our inertial navigation systems are within tolerance and navigating properly. More monitoring.

Then there's the fuel. It has to be balanced as it burns, and that involves cross-feeds and boost pumps. You also have to watch the temperature and keep it from gelling when it gets too cold. As the fuel burns off, your plane is lighter and you need to climb because a jet engine is more efficient at high altitudes.

Rarely is a flight uneventful from preflight to landing. The weather in Tokyo may be good, but that doesn't mean that it will stay that way. Also, winds can be stronger than forecast, so we're always ready to divert. Some days, when there are no auto throttles, we can't take our eyes off the mach meter for two seconds without having to adjust the throttles. Or the fuel keeps getting off balance because one of the engines is burning more for some reason.

Don't get me wrong. We can and do relax up there. We just don't get bored. Not really. Our backs get sore, our buttocks get numb, and we need to exercise. Yes, we get tired, but that's par for the course with any job. I actually get less tired when lots of little things are going wrong and keep me busy.

I think all jobs seem easier the longer you do them. Complacency can set in if you let it. Cargo is fairly routine, unless there is a mechanical problem with the plane... or an unruly zebra trying to kick its way out of a crate. Passenger flights are less predictable. There are always medical problems or rowdy, misbehaving people, making us ask, "Should we call Mayo Clinic? Should we divert and land?"

Real fatigue sets in after an emergency. One day, flying from Tokyo to Seattle, our upper deck flight attendant collapsed. She was having heart problems and struggling to breathe. A doctor on board said she was unstable and needed to get to a hospital as soon as possible. We were over the middle of the Pacific, four hours from anywhere. She might not make it, the doctor said.

Okay, so maybe we get bored sometimes while en route…

For the next three hours and forty-five minutes we stepped over her to go to the bathroom. It was nerve wracking. We knew this woman. We liked her. *We didn't want her to die.*

After landing in Anchorage, an ambulance met the flight and we refueled. Another passenger was having heart problems and needed to be taken off. Then we had to find his bags. Finally, we took off to Seattle. About halfway there, I realized I was exhausted. When you're on an adrenaline high, your body can only sustain it for so long. We tumbled into our beds in Seattle, as tired as I'd ever been. Next time, I decided, we would shut the flight down in Anchorage, for safety.

Of course takeoffs and landings are the most challenging and fun. But cruise flight is, well, cruising. You kick back, relax and watch the clouds go by. We sip our coffee and munch our croissants. Drinking fresh squeezed orange juice, watching the sun come up over the South China Sea—this is the life. Clouds reflect in the glassy water below and seem to just hang there. Thunderstorms grow to thousands of feet before our eyes.

The cockpit is like an office—our office. We keep an eye on the radar and the horizon for thunderstorms. The banter between us, as well as small mechanical incidents, pass the time. We have revisions to do and developments in aviation to keep up on. The time passes more quickly than you might think. Sometimes we have to solve each other's marital problems. Playing 'Dear Abby' or 'Dr. Laura' keeps us busy!

Meanwhile, the world goes by beneath us: The Great Wall of China, the glaciers of Alaska, the cinder cones of Kamchatka, the Marianas Trench. Did you know that, flying over the Marianas Trench at 36,000 feet, you are really at 72,000? Fourteen miles above land! The ocean there is the deepest in the world. The trench is where the vent worms live without light, digesting the gases from inside the earth.

There is so much to see if you know where to look. Sometimes you can see the Aleutian Islands and fishing boats. The patterns on the water are mesmerizing, but mostly we are too high to see much detail. You can see the San Andreas Fault in California. At night there are always shooting stars and, sometimes, Northern Lights.

The fishing boat fleets look like constellations. It is surprising to me that there are still fish in the sea. Between geology, astronomy, and geography, there is plenty to keep your mind occupied.

The islands around southern parts of Japan are beautiful. I wondered aloud why they weren't tourist destinations. "Sea snakes," the captain told me, "poisonous sea snakes." Most of the guys I flew with were stationed in this part of the world and had amazing stories. They all had different interests and hobbies. Some were armchair historians, others were geologists. I can't begin to tell you all that they have taught me.

Some of the pilots were in Vietnam when Jane Fonda came over to protest the war—sympathizing with North Vietnam and telling the North Vietnamese that most of the United States did not want the war. Their friends were either tortured after her visit or killed. Instead of being treated like prisoners of war they were branded as *traitors*. Listening to their stories explained much. No wonder they didn't think she should be woman of the year!

They also told me that I was taking a job meant for a veteran who had served his country. I explained, repeatedly, that my father and stepfather died young, of service-connected causes. My current stepfather had his leg blown apart by a piece of exploding shrapnel. That's enough, most of them conceded.

Talking fills hours of time. Equally time consuming are the hours we spent diverting around weather. Our radar is helpful, but not enough. Other pilot reports, as well as winds aloft, help determine how far we need to deviate around thunderstorms. Often it was hard to get a clearance because the only communication we have is through HF (high frequency) radios. Sometimes it took forty minutes to get in touch with someone on the ground.

The static and foreign dialects are always a challenge. It's like talking through coffee cans. The voices are tinny and hard to understand. No, flying in this part of the world isn't as boring as it is tedious. The women's voices in Taipei are the worst. No, wait, Bangkok is a close second. Apparently the microphones are set for the lower voice frequency that most men have. Some female voices sound like chalk on a blackboard as they screech at you. It gives us something to talk about, though, and it is hard to be bored when you can't understand a word they're saying.

Don't misunderstand me. I'm eternally grateful that English is the international language. It must be difficult to learn it well enough to use in a technical profession. We have difficulty flying into Japan with an emergency because, even though the controllers speak English, it is very basic. Anything out of the ordinary will not be understood. They understand "emergency," "fire," and a few other terms. "We're having problems with our landing gear" is not in their English vocabulary.

Shanghai and Beijing China are my least favorite destinations to fly into. All the other planes in the sky are speaking Chinese, the visibility is usually low due to smog, and I have no idea where all the traffic is. Being able to listen to the controller give another plane instructions in our language is invaluable. I've heard controllers clear planes to our altitude and airspace while in a holding pattern in China and Japan. I query them and there is a loud, sucking-through-the-teeth noise as they quickly have you descend. Flying is not boring and you had better be awake.

It amazes me that we are so fair and welcoming to airlines from other countries, but foreign controllers aren't welcoming to us. Our controllers are professional and they receive planes on a first come, first serve, basis unless there is an emergency. In Japan, Japanese airliners receive priority treatment over us and it is not unusual to have them squeeze three of their flights in front of us! Coming from the United States we carry a limited amount of fuel. As soon as we have unforeseen weather or holding, we have to think of contingency plans. Will we divert to Yokota or Haneda?

Often, flying into Narita, Japan we are instructed to hold. There are too many heavy airplanes for an airport with one long runway, and there is only one flight pattern used for each direction. There are no visual approaches, and even if you are the only plane in the sky you will be vectored miles away before they turn you in to final approach. This uses a lot of fuel.

One day we had been holding for forty minutes. A jet burns more fuel at lower altitudes, and even though we were lighter than we were ten hours ago, we still burn at least 20,000 pounds an hour. We usually arrive with 30,000 pounds, so we didn't have much to spare. Just as we were discussing diverting the controller gave us vectors to the runway. We put out flaps, which slow us down but also burn more fuel because of drag. Then the controller started putting Japanese airplanes in front of us.

I protested and told him we need to land or divert to Haneda.

"Are you declaring emergency?"

"No, but what is our sequence?" This is Japan. Our "sequence" is whatever they decide it will be depending on their mood. It is frustrating and unprofessional. Our carrier made the Japanese paper regularly because, as Americans, we weren't afraid of 'losing face.' If we were low on fuel, we told them. That would not happen on a Japanese airliner... They would never admit it.

I know the world isn't fair, but sometimes I just get tired of it. When we flew over Russia and used their airspace, we paid them $7,000 *an hour*. They use our airspace for free. Landing fees in the United States are a fraction of what they are elsewhere in the world. In the late 90s, we heard that Japan charged $11,000 a landing at Osaka's Kansai International Airport and they wanted to raise it to $13,000 because it was sinking and they had to fix it. Narita charged $9,000 a landing and $7,000 to overnight! Los Angeles, on the other hand, had just raised theirs to a whopping $2,000.

I think excitement is overrated. You can't be happy and excited every moment of your life. If you need immediate highs and get bored easily, reevaluate your priorities and needs. It isn't realistic to think any career can provide a constant excitement and you are setting yourself up for disappointment.

If I was stateside after flying all night I'd take a nap, then take a walk and go to a nice restaurant that might cost more but felt like a treat—a French restaurant overlooking the wharf in Seattle or the deck of a five-star hotel on the beach near Beverly Hills. It takes work to pull yourself out of a crabby mood when you've been away from home for over a week and are exhausted.

Sometimes the job was tedious and I got jet lagged, tired, and cranky. That's when I slept and nurtured myself. Prices for massage and foot reflexology are quite reasonable in Asia, as long as you aren't in Japan.

Some months I chose a long Hong Kong layover and took the double decker bus over to Stanley Market to shop, read, and people watch. Other months I would choose Guam or Saipan! I flew to places I only dreamed of when growing up. As a child, my grandparents traveled to Europe and brought me souvenirs. A friend of my mother's went to Japan and brought me a parasol and clogs, then a beautiful doll from China. Oh, to be able to travel like that! My favorite story book had pictures of faraway places. My sixth grade teacher taught social studies with a vengeance. When we finished our class work we could read her collection of huge, colorful fairy tales from around the world.

Singapore was just a mythical rain forest city at the end of the world, to me. The first time I went there, I bought a Sunset travel book and memorized it for our three-day stay. The guys joked that I was better than a travel agent. Little India, Chinatown, Arab Street—we saw them all. We hired a bumboat to take us on a tour of the harbor. Sipping our Singha beer we motored past humongous tankers from Romania and Lithuania and places I had never heard of. We toured an island with a Chinese temple and golfed on Sentosa. *You don't retrieve your ball if it goes into the rough because there are poisonous snakes.* Monkeys chattered above us in the trees and cockatoos flew over our heads. I'd only seen cockatoos in pet stores.

Boring. Does life get boring to you? Sometimes mine lacks variety, or seems like an uphill battle. I slog along, forgetting how good I have it. I think that, without major adversity like poverty or war, I lose my perspective and forget to be grateful. I appreciated home more with my job than I would have with an eight to five schedule. I enjoyed hotel rooms, but I love to sleep in my own bed and snuggle with my husband. I feel so blessed to do what I do and be where I am.

Excitement and boredom are the extremes.
I'll take the middle road.

Kevin and me on a cruise through Tahiti.

DANGER

I met an FAA inspector at Little Rock Airport while flying my Cessna 140 from Colorado to Florida. At first I thought he was looking for me, but I knew I had closed my flight plan after landing in the farmer's field. He was waiting for an overdue pilot on his first solo cross country flight. We chatted for a few minutes, and I told him where I was headed.

"I investigated an accident in Gainesville last year," he said. "A preacher and his family were flying IFR (Instrument Flying Rules) without a clearance and lightning struck the Bonanza, shearing the tail." My mouth dropped open. When I was a receptionist in high school the preacher would fly every Sunday, no matter what the weather was. He would brag about busting minimums to get home from his sermons, and said God was his copilot. I wondered how long he could get away with his actions. Four years later, I knew. As the saying goes…

There are old pilots and there are bold pilots, but there are no old, bold pilots. Aviation in itself is not dangerous, but it inherently unforgiving of any carelessness or neglect.

ONE NIGHT, OVER the Colorado Rockies monitoring the cloud seeding, I was a passenger and my ex-husband was logging free multi-engine time. My ex came back to the cabin to take a sample. When he returned to the right seat in the cockpit, the captain confided that he was lost because he hadn't flown IFR in a long time. We were in a bad place to be lost, near Pike's Peak, at minimum altitude for the sampling. Some of the peaks were above us. From then on, I took the samples while my ex flew the plane.

Another time, flying into Boise, Idaho for the Forest Service, it was my leg—my turn to fly. The captain said he had the runway lights at 200 feet, but advised me to stay on the gauges and not look up because the snow flurries were disorientating. Even at 100 feet, runway in sight, he told me to stay on the instruments. His next call was, "Flare." *I did.* We couldn't see to taxi in and the tower couldn't see us. I was angry. I realized the field was below minimums and we had just landed. The captain admitted he had never seen anything—no lights, no runway, until we were less than fifty feet! The captain's 'get-home-itis' could have killed us. Once the 'Follow Me Truck' found us, we followed it to the ramp because we couldn't see to taxi.

When you fly with a pilot who displays poor judgment, you have to stand up for your life. I guess that's how you learn, if you don't die first. Teaching flying, I was the conservative one. I didn't take chances, and for good reason: I had already lost too many friends in accidents that could have been avoided. One of my friends was what I would call an 'ace.' He was an excellent pilot who had flown Lear jets for Clay Lacey out of California. Flying a twin-engine home to Klamath Falls one night, he lost his gyros over the Willamette Valley. Seattle Center urged him to land at

Portland International. He elected to continue on. He had a wife and baby and was eager to get home to them. 'Get-Home-Itis' is a deadly disease. He iced up and spun in over the Columbia Gorge.

IT'S TRUE. AVIATION isn't scary. You just have to be careful. Airline flying is even safer. The 747 has four engines, four hydraulic systems, four electrical generators—four of everything, with backups to the backups. Boeing builds strong, reliable tanks. They performed structural tests on the wings using a forklift to bend them until they break. The wings didn't break until they were almost vertical—more Gs than the human body can take.

Turbulence didn't bother me. If I was on my break and there was no severe weather ahead, I loved it. To me, turbulence was like being in a rocking chair. I knew the plane could handle it, and if it got really bad, I'd put on my seatbelt so I couldn't fall out of my bunk, and then sleep like a baby.

Some of the flights where I should have been scared, I was too busy to think about being afraid. One time we lost an engine on the way to Narita and radioed our operations. They didn't want us to continue to Tokyo—the dispatcher said we didn't have enough fuel with the forecast winds. We knew we did, but decided they were afraid of the bad press the Japanese government gives us. So, we diverted to Hong Kong like they requested.

Unfortunately, we were just north of Taipei, and getting onto the A1, the main airway, was impossible. Taipei Control vectored us even farther north, because the traffic was too heavy and they were trying to fit us in. By the time we neared Hong Kong, our fuel was low and the weather was closing in. We made an approach to minimums and landed, but we were sweating bullets. It was nerve wracking knowing that we *had* to land—we couldn't go around or go to an alternate because we didn't have enough kerosene. It took them three days to fix the freighter, and I needed that time to recuperate. Close calls wear me out.

I'm just glad to be an old pilot.

Narita, Japan rice fields.

STAYING ALIVE

The closest I ever came to dying was on a flight to Narita, Japan. The winds were strong and gusty, with wind shear at the field. On final approach, the captain was having trouble controlling the plane. The flight engineer and I were calling out airspeeds and altitudes. It got violent and scary. We told the captain to go around. *He wouldn't.*

The airplane in front of us reported severe wind shear, decided not to land, and requested vectors to Haneda—Tokyo's other airport. Narita International was effectively closed down. Silently the engineer and I cheered. We were going to Haneda, too! The captain had other ideas. We had enough fuel to go into a holding pattern and wait for the winds to die down. The flight engineer and I protested, to no avail. The captain promised us that if it was still bad on the next approach, we would go to our alternate airport. Twenty minutes later, we tried again.

It seemed impossible, but it was worse than before. The plane was thrown around the sky like a toy boat on the ocean. Encountering wind shear at five hundred feet, we told him to go around. I started to push the power up, but the captain shook his head and pushed my hand away. Short of committing mutiny, there was nothing I could do. At two hundred feet above the ground, the plane rolled sideways, out of control. I looked out my window at the pavement below. I knew I was dead, just like a friend who lost his life in a Lear jet. We would cartwheel and burn. I hoped it would be quick, and said a silent prayer and goodbye to my family. Miraculously, the plane righted and the captain squeaked the wheels onto the runway. *A perfect touchdown.*

The passengers cheered. The engineer and I were furious. The captain was apologetic, but claimed he knew what he was doing. *Bullshit.* We taxied to the gate. We were the only plane that landed in Narita that afternoon.

Twenty-seven other flights diverted to Haneda. We reported the captain to Professional Standards. Instead of being in trouble with the company, we received letters of commendation. *Unbelievable.*

The engineer quit the airline to live out his days on his boat. I pondered what else I could have done. To this day I am convinced the engineer and I should have been more forceful, but I know we wouldn't have a job if we had pushed the issue.

Don't get talked into something you don't want to do. It could be your last mistake.

A guard at the Narita International Airport in Japan.

FLIGHT ATTENDANTS

"So, how do you get along with the flight attendants?" people ask. They assume the flight attendants see me as either a threat or a competitor.

I got along great with the flight attendants. I respected them and they respected me. Most of the flight attendants were my biggest fans. They bragged to the passengers and congratulated me when I introduced myself before a flight. When I greased the landing, I was the star on the bus ride to the terminal or the hotel. It was funny because, to them, my achievement was their achievement. *And it was.*

Sure, I've had a few problems over the years. Occasionally, other female pilots had treated them poorly, so the jury was out until they got to know me. Sometimes the flight attendants weren't comfortable with women pilots, especially if they were a little afraid of flying. Or if the men told them women were not as good and they believed it. Some of the flight attendants didn't think they could do the job, so they didn't believe I could, either.

Early on, flying the Boeing 727, being a female pilot was a huge novelty. The flight attendants were always asking me questions they never could ask the male pilots. They wanted to know more about the plane, the weather, instrument approaches, anything and everything—but they didn't want to appear stupid. They knew I wouldn't laugh at them.

"Could you show us what you look for when you walk around the airplane?" four of them asked one day. We were on a three-day trip with lots of time to talk. They followed me on my preflight around the Boeing 727. The male pilots shook their heads and laughed, saying, "None of the flight attendants follow us around on preflights."

"You would be so pretty if you wore makeup," flight attendants used to tell me. *Now how do I respond to that?* I would say, "But I do have makeup on." Not enough, was their answer, and then they would give me makeup lessons on layovers. I really didn't know much about dressing and being a girl—I had spent too many years with men. I didn't have money to spend on "girl things" when I was younger because all my money went towards flying. Again, the flight attendants took me under their wings.

I do have to be careful what I wear for makeup in flight. Hair spray and oil based cosmetics are ignited by oxygen. Wouldn't that be bad in an emergency? As soon as I put on my oxygen mask, my face *ignites*!

On layovers I'd go out with the flight attendants as often as I did with the pilots. Knowing the latest beauty and fashion trends, they were great to shop with, especially in Asia. Pearls, purses, and designer clothes at the lowest prices were their specialty. Besides, after being with the guys in the cockpit all day, I needed girl time.

One day a flight attendant came up to the cockpit asking for "a guy" to come down and help her. She apologized to me, but said it had to be one of the guys. They were both busy, and it was my job as a flight engineer to handle cabin problems. "No, really, it's too hard and too heavy for you," she protested. I insisted that I would come back and get one of them if I couldn't handle it.

I followed her downstairs. None of the flight attendants were happy to see me instead of a strong guy and they made that clear when I walked into the mid-galley. The caterers had loaded a carrier in the wrong position. It had to be switched with one below. "See. I told you we need one of the guys," she said.

I knew what to do—I just didn't know how to do it without making them feel stupid. *Yes, they were too heavy for me to lift and move.* Taking a deep breath, I took the racks of glasses out one by one. Then I emptied the bottles out of the bottom carrier. Pulling the empty carriers out, I switched them. Then I put the glasses and bottles back in.

One of the girls rolled her eyes and said, "That's why she gets paid the big bucks. She uses her brain." Everyone laughed and the tension was broken.

Another time I was deadheading home and the only available seat was the flight attendant jump seat in first class. The flight attendant was extremely busy and I offered to help. She started giving me jobs, like opening wine. Then I helped do the meal set-up.

I thought I was doing a good job, but I had to ask where things were and how to do tasks that were unfamiliar. "Don't you ever work this airplane?" she asked, harried and annoyed.

"All the time, but on the other side of the door." *She hadn't heard me say I was a pilot.*

"Oh my gosh, I'm so sorry! Sit down, you don't have to help. I thought you were a flight attendant!" Her face turned bright red.

I told her I didn't mind helping, if I really was helping. But if I was in her way... She needed the help, so we finished the service together, dumb questions and all.

Some of my best layovers have been with flight attendants, and they had the best room parties. It is great to be with other women and share experiences and stories you would never discuss with men. The conversations include gas, farting, belching, constipation, cramps, PMS, pregnancy, nursing, and menopause. Did you know flight attendants often miscarry their first pregnancy?

Women are great for support and caring, and I beg to disagree with women who prefer the company of men. They just haven't found the *right* women. My women friends are worth their weight in gold. When I flew out of Chicago to Tokyo, I became good friends with quite a few flight attendants. We were always joking around, and they were usually pulling pranks on the pilots. The old days, before sexual harassment, were more fun in some ways. The jokes were better and you didn't worry about offending people. We laughed more. I liked the joke, "What's the difference between a cactus and a cockpit?" *On a cactus, the pricks are on the outside.*

My girlfriend Ellen came up one day, reading a joke book I had brought with me, and asked the guys if they knew what married men who fooled around and oysters had in common. They shook their heads. (She knew both men were having affairs.) "They're both full of slime, but one in a million has a pearl inside." The guys decided they were both one in a million, and we cracked up.

I don't fool around with the flight attendants. Or pilots, for that matter. But the stories are true. Body shots on the bar, guys doing the "walk of shame" back to their rooms at four in the morning, affairs that go on for years—all true. Being away from home gets old, and if you let nature take its course, the inevitable happens.

The strangest affair I've been privy to was between a male captain and female copilot. I knew them both, and I knew their spouses. I couldn't figure out why the copilot was getting so upset with me for joking with the captain and asking about his wife. Finally, after a long, uncomfortable week we were walking to dinner. She grabbed his buttocks and said, "Oh. You're really not wearing any underwear, are you?" The evening progressed, and they got drunk and less careful about what I saw. I excused myself and went back to the hotel, feeling like a naive idiot.

They came back to the hotel sometime later, and I heard them in the hall. Through the peephole, I saw them laughing and hanging on each other as they went into the room next to mine. Any doubts I had were answered—the walls were thin.

We were all deadheading home the next day—he and I on one flight, she on another. He told me his wife had something planned that afternoon, and he was angry because she knew how tired he was after a trip. I was tired of being played for a fool, and I felt bad for his wife. "It's not Jan's fault you didn't get any sleep last night," I responded.

He looked at me, surprised I knew, and then mumbled, "You're right. You're right, you're right, you're right."

Should I have said anything? Probably not. It was none of my business. But my ex-husband fooled around on me all the time. The odd phone calls, the hang ups, the accusations, the venereal disease, and basic lack of honesty—I finally figured it out. It was as if someone turned the lights on: my ex had picked fights with me because he felt guilty and was trying to justify what he had done.

THE NEW 747-400s came along and the older passenger models were sold. As much as I loved the flight attendants, flying freight was easier. We could push back and start engines whenever we were ready. When we were hungry or thirsty, we got up and served ourselves. We didn't worry about getting in anyone's way, or starving until they had time to feed us. There were no hassles and no landings for medical emergencies. Occasionally, I saw girlfriends on layovers in Japan or on one of our few passenger flights in the two 747s configured for people. The airline had thousands of flight attendants and pilots, so our paths still crossed sporadically.

I missed the good old days when the airline was smaller and we flew together all month. We weren't as tired because the schedules were more humane with humans designing them instead of computers, and we were younger and more energetic. We had longer layovers, and there was more time for camaraderie.

Flight Attendants are some of my best friends.

Kathleen Hatfield and I toured Singapore on a three-day layover.
We did it all!

WOMEN IN AVIATION

Flying an airplane that seats over 400 people may seem daunting, but no one flies a big jet initially. Like everything else, it's a step by step process. First I learned to fly a little two seat Cessna, then I moved up to a bigger engine and two more seats. Next I flew planes with constant speed propellers and retractable landing gear, then more horsepower and speed. Instrument flying was a whole new skill set, as was multi-engine flight. Slowly, deliberately, I learned to fly more complicated planes until, eventually, I was flying a 747.

I think my college classes prepared me for the logical thinking and memorization, but I don't think I was smarter than anyone else. My grades in high school were As and Bs and my grades in college weren't stellar—no matter how hard I tried. It didn't help that many of my courses were pre-med, and I could have been an A student with an easier major. My GPA was only a 3.1 when I graduated.

I would label myself as someone of normal intelligence with *abnormal* stick-to-it-iveness. Maybe I'm not giving myself enough credit, but I don't think that's the case. Most of my girlfriends could have become pilots with the right amount of training. They might not have enjoyed it like I did, but they are intelligent enough to fly a plane.

The skills it takes to be a pilot are skills all successful mothers have. Women need to stop selling themselves short and keep track of what they do well, like waking up each day to get the kids ready for school, keeping the house clean (enough), and putting food on the table. Homework hassles and ordinary life aren't easy—ask anyone whose parents weren't there for them.

None of my girlfriends would have any trouble competing with a college kid for a job. They're all competent and capable, having raised their children and handled their lives well. The only problem is that they don't believe in themselves. They still lack self-confidence after years of successful living.

Instead of patting ourselves and each other on the back for all that we've done well, we let our doubts and fears take over. Perhaps we've realized how much luck has played in it all. Luck seems an iffy way to live.

Life can turn on a dime. One of my close friends lost her son, another friend lost her career, and yet another lost both. Instead of being safe and predictable, life appears to be a big crapshoot. We're playing Russian roulette with a loaded gun. It's scary, I guess, if you let yourself think that way, but for me the uncertainty has always been part of the whole.

Men and women need each other in this world, as equal partners. Together we balance each other out. I know many of the men I worked with thought less of me because I put my family before my career. It validated their theory that you can't or shouldn't be both a mother and a pilot. I haven't missed a Christmas with my family and I think that's a coup. I planned it that way. Sure, a day is just a day, but I didn't miss my kids' birthdays, either.

Staying senior has cost me plenty. I always said it didn't matter; that if I had trouble checking out after being a flight engineer so long, so be it. *But it did matter.* I wanted to excel at both flying and family.

When I was in my twenties, no one could buffalo me. The examiner who signed me off to fly flight engineer on the Boeing 727 gave me a five-hour test when everyone else's test was two hours. I passed, but it was grueling and my first taste of real inequality. It only made me more determined.

As the years went on, life began to take its toll. Always having to prove myself got old. Check rides became something to dread. Male or female, we all know that you can take check rides that are impossible to pass. All the examiner has to do is overload us or get us preoccupied while he throws in another problem. Sure enough, we will have trouble passing. Well, try getting through when the odds are against you and no one believes in you. It's almost like trying to be superhuman. No, I didn't flunk my check rides, but I know women who always busted their first one before passing the second one. Don't tell me that is a good, confidence-building strategy.

I took an art class with a lady whose brother was an airline pilot. He told her none of the female pilots were any good. I asked her if she believed him. She said he was a good pilot and she did! That tells me she didn't have confidence in herself, either.

A woman pilot I know said there were no good female pilots on the 747. She thinks she's good, of course, but the guys tell her stories about the other females, so she believed none of the rest of us were any good. *How sad is it to buy into thinking like that?* Until we have enough women pilots in aviation, we won't reach the tipping point necessary for thoughts like that to change. Someday...

When women don't believe in each other, it's sad.

PICK A PATH, ANY PATH

There are many paths that I could have chosen. All of them would have been the right path for me. There are always signs, no matter which path you choose—so you can't always interpret a sign as meaning you're still on the 'right path' or the wrong one. You have to be careful not to see everything as a sign that you should be going in a different direction. It isn't so much *what* you do as *how* you live your life.

Most of my friends had no idea what they wanted to be when they grew up, any more than I did. Now I realize that, even in high school, my interests and likes were already well established. If I had paid attention to who I already was, I would have had all the answers I needed.

I loved arts and crafts. I still do. I thought about being an occupational therapist. The hospital therapy department where I interned in the twelfth grade was a treasure trove. Their art supplies included a potter's wheel, a printing press, everything necessary for leather and copper tooling, painting and drawing supplies, and silk screening. It was a dream come true to use such a well-stocked art room.

My stepfather considered it playtime. He had had polio and occupational therapy was a huge part of his recovery, yet he considered it a waste of time. Maybe for him, it was. But I saw 'playtime' improve the lives of many patients. It involved so much more than arts and crafts. There was the little girl who was dying of leukemia but wanted to finish leather wallets for all her family first. There was the burn victim who needed the special implements we supplied to help her eat and function, and the psych patients who needed the creative time to unwind. It would have been a great career for me.

Architecture and interior design caught and held my interest for years, as I explained earlier. I fantasized about being the next Frank Lloyd Wright, since I was sure we were related.

Mom was frustrated with her field. She was being paid half of what men in her specialty earned, and had been for years. The University of Florida sent out a query letter insisting that they did not discriminate and if you knew any male doing your job and making more, let them know. Mom knew the man in the office down the hall was making twice her salary as a Professor of Audiology; she knew that she was also supervising the Preschool Deaf Program and had graduate students. She responded to their letter.

Her next paycheck was doubled. There was no explanation or apology. She was never awarded back pay nor was she paid appropriately for her current duties. I think this jaded her opinion of the field at the time. She told me not to go into her profession. At the time, it hurt my feelings because I thought she didn't want me as an equal or as a peer. Now I know that she was trying to protect me.

So, what would I be? I loved to travel. I was an explorer and an adventurer. My childhood was spent building forts and hideaways. The summer we spent on an island in northern Ontario fishing and swimming to our heart's content was wonderful. And the beaches of Florida… there was nothing I liked better than beachcombing and studying ocean life. I thought about marine biology. I had a good command of the French language, both written and spoken; Jacques Cousteau might hire me on his boat, The Calypso.

"Another overcrowded field. You'll never make it in that," well-meaning adults counseled me.

I was clueless, drifting, and unsure. Or so I thought. I already had some big pieces of my puzzle put together and just didn't know it. Children, exploring, traveling, arts and crafts, reading, writing, swimming, beachcombing, interior decorating, learning anything new, and flying. Thirty-plus years later I still enjoy them all. The foundation was already in place, unbeknownst to me. Over the years I have added to them, falling in love with photography, drawing and painting, and working with glass.

Too many pilots I know are burned out. They don't like to fly. They hate teaching and they hate their commuter jobs. Everything they had to do to get to the pinnacle, an airline job, was an ordeal instead of an adventure. All they could think about was the airline job because that was their dream. To them, being an airline pilot meant they could live anywhere in the world, have most of the month off, and make over two hundred thousand a year doing what they love. Of course this is all perception and not reality. You can live anywhere in the world if you have the seniority to bid schedules that allow you to get your flying done in consecutive days. At times during my career I've only had to work nine days a month, but I did that by foregoing pay raises and staying in a lower flying position than my classmates. And yes, after working as an airline pilot for twenty-three years, I made over $240,000 a year.

Then we had to take pay cuts of forty percent or more. Our pension plan was in jeopardy. Our benefits were being cut, and the job was not what it used to be. The trips were more work with less time off. Commuting to work was not easy with full airplanes and canceled flights. But if you loved the flying and traveling like I did, the job was still ideal.

Each month I chose where I wanted to fly. Often I chose Singapore, a magical place to me—a place in fairy tales and story books. I learned about 'The Lion City' in the sixth grade, but never dreamed I could go there every month.

Boat Quay, Singapore.

Culture and history surrounded me, and it was thrilling to be at the equator. I loved the food, the animals, the feel of the place—everything! I would hop a bus to Malaysia or a ferry to Indonesia when I wanted a change.

Hong Kong was another favorite destination of mine. At first layovers there were daunting. The city is crowded and poverty is rampant. The harbor smells like a sewer, giving new meaning to the name Hong Kong or fragrant harbor. Why would anyone want to live here, much less visit or vacation? Once I knew what to expect,

I loved going there, too. The latest high-rise buildings are architectural marvels. Dragon boats and junks traverse the South China Sea amidst giant tankers while expensive cars, taxis, and rickshaws filled the streets. I wasn't just in another country; I was in another world. There were so many contrasts and the culture was different from anywhere else on the globe.

Hong Kong Harbor.

I love a challenge. Flying is hard work, especially with typhoons, wind shear, ocean crossings, and emergencies. It's all part of the job. If I didn't have forces of nature and mechanical problems to contend with, my job would be boring.

Every time I went to work, walking onto the ramp toward my airplane, I was in awe. The 747 is the length of a football field and has a takeoff weight of over 400 tons. I can't believe I flew something this incredible.

I sometimes wonder what I would be doing had well-meaning adults not discouraged me from so many of my other career choices. I doubt they would have swayed me if I had been more sure of what I wanted. Their experiences and disappointments did not have to be mine. But eventually I stumbled onto a career I loved. Thirty years later I still enjoyed my job and my lifestyle.

No, there isn't just one path for anyone. I don't even believe there are wrong choices, just some that make your life better or easier than others. I think there are "many right ways to do the same thing" and many roads leading to the same place. But you'll never get anywhere if you don't start down a path.

Pick a path, don't look back, and enjoy the journey.

CAPTAIN 747

12 1 747 ANC NRT 907 0500 0740 840 840 840 1010 3120 3250 RADISSON HOTEL

Who would have thought I would be a 747 captain? Watching the gigantic military aircraft take off from the Dover Air Force Base as a child, I never dreamed I would be a pilot.

Taking a deep breath, I push the fistful of throttles toward the stops, almost all the way forward. My heart races as the airspeed indicator begins to move.

The copilot calls out the speeds. "60 knots."

Weighing over 830,000 pounds, my 747 lumbers down the runway. *The Whale.* Most people think about a huge animal swimming through the sea when they hear the term. My whale's shape is the same, and the smooth, laminar flow of air around it is like water. But today it also feels like a whale—very heavy and cumbersome.

"80 knots."

I love this airplane, especially on takeoff with the accompanying adrenaline rush and feeling of power. Sometimes I feel like rocking back and forth in my seat, like pumping a swing, to help it build up speed. There are days we wonder aloud if we will clear the end of the runway, even with four engines at full thrust.

"100."

"120/V1."

V1 is our stop or go speed. Before V1, we would have enough pavement to stop even if an engine fails or a moose runs on the runway. *Theoretically.* Who knows if we really could. Not long ago, a 747 went right off the end onto the highway at Anchorage International. I take my hand off the throttles and place it on the control wheel.

Now we are committed, even if we lose an engine. Taking my hand off the throttles prevents me from inadvertently pulling them back in an emergency.

The end of the runway is approaching fast as our 747 still struggles to gain enough speed. Some days I wish they would make runways a mile longer, and today is one of them.

"Rotate, 13 degrees."

I pull back on the heavy wheel. A simulator can't imitate this real life *feeling* of whether or not the airplane is ready to fly. This 747, an old freighter-bomber model, doesn't exactly leap off the runway. But it does climb, albeit at a slower rate than I am used to. Roaring into the sky just after five a.m., a gigantic smile spreads across my face.

The three of us scan the area for traffic. This is a busy corridor, an area full of general aviation floatplanes and tail-draggers flying under visual flight rules. We are so slow and heavy today that our exposure is greater than usual—it takes us longer to climb through this congested area. The tower operator informs us of traffic at twelve o'clock and two o'clock, but we don't see them. ATC radar doesn't always paint the smaller, fabric-covered planes, either. Hopefully, they will see and avoid us, and vice versa. We keep looking.

Some people claim takeoff is the most dangerous part of the flight, and they are right. We are climbing at a relatively low airspeed and higher angle of attack. We are very heavy, and if we should lose an engine, we will be very busy. With each engine producing over 58,000 pounds of thrust, losing an outboard engine—at the tip of the wing—means the same engine on the other side will try to roll or tip the plane. I would have to lower the nose—because I have less lift and need to fly faster—and turn or "bank" into the good engine. The copilot and flight engineer would be busy, too. They would be running through a checklist, trying to secure the failed engine and make sure it isn't on fire. We might try to restart the engine, but if a restart isn't possible, we would be dumping fuel and returning to the airport we took off from, as long as the weather is still favorable.

To me, takeoff and landing are the best parts. I love being busy and I love hand flying. Autopilots are great for straight and level flight, but this is why I became a pilot—for the fun of flying. This is what we are trained to do, and it is all routine to us.

Calmly, we do our jobs and survey the beauty of Alaska that surrounds us. This Great Land, with all of its mountains and glaciers, is amazing to behold from the air. The controller gives us a vector away from the mountains, since our climb rate is too slow to go over them yet. Small planes are still everywhere, and we keep our eyes peeled. It's a lot different than 9/11 when we were the only plane in the sky.

I glance up at the circuit breaker panel above my head when I hear a distinct "pop." The engineer hears it, too, and reaches up to push it back in. He leaps back in shock as it sputters as sparks shoot out. "Let's not reset that again," I say. "Are you okay?" He nods, but it is obvious that has never happened to him before. It reminds me of another freighter flight, an almost flight, when there really were flames coming out of the instrument panel. So many memories—such a great career.

I made it!

Me, with four stripes, a real captain, holding my airplane!

JUST SHOOT ME

I always said you would have to shoot me to get me out of my airline job before retirement age. Well, God did.

I don't know when my boundless store of energy began to leave me, or when I quit being as excited to go to Singapore, Hong Kong, and Amsterdam. I only know that instead of hitting the ground running, I spent more time by the pool or in my bed. I told myself I was getting older, but it bothered me that I couldn't pull out more enthusiasm. I felt like an old clock running down. I began to wish I were independently wealthy so I didn't have to fly anymore. I wished for a sabbatical. The jet lag was getting to me, I thought. Damn. I liked being the Energizer Bunny.

Flying into Hong Kong late one night I noticed I couldn't read the approach plate. Even the new Hong Kong airport is tricky, with lots of speed restrictions to adhere to and particular points where you begin descents and carefully orchestrated maneuvers to avoid the peaks nearby. It is dangerous not to be able to read the instructions, and I would have been worried if I were unfamiliar with the approach to this runway. However, our annual check ride used this very scenario, and I had it memorized. What did worry me was that I could see all the letters and numbers in front of me, but there were gaps and nonsensical words. It seemed my brain was not interpreting what my eye was reading.

Two more times that week I noticed visual discrepancies. They were in my hotel room, on the ground and not the cockpit, but still, it was scary. I called my doctor from Korea and he was concerned enough to schedule me for tests. Upon my return to the states, I stopped at The Dalles and went to the hospital for magnetic resonance imagery (MRI) of my head. Then I drove home.

A flight attendant told me to do a cleanse to enhance my energy. I bought the products she sold, and started on them the next day. I always feel sick with cleanses. I'm told the flu-like symptoms is your body getting rid of toxins. This one worked so well that I woke up at midnight with severe stomach pain. I looked up the ingredients on the internet. There was nothing I had not taken before or that I knew I was allergic to. I stopped the cleanse, but the pain continued.

My husband said the stomach flu was going around—he had it while I was gone. I found it hard to believe this was just the flu, but what else could it be? I spent a couple days in pain. Finally, I couldn't take it any longer. At five a.m. I woke my husband and told him I needed to go to the hospital.

"For the stomach flu?" he exclaimed, disbelieving.

"If this is the stomach flu, then I'm a wimp, but I can't take the pain any longer."

"Okay, I'll drive you in as soon as we get Colt off to school," Kevin said.

"No, let him get himself ready. I need to go now."

Shaking his head, my husband drove me in.

Of course, it wasn't the stomach flu. My white blood count was off the charts high, and a CAT, (computed axial tomography) scan showed my appendix was white and thready. The surgeon, Dr. Moon, asked me when I last ate. I told him I hadn't eaten since yesterday—nothing this morning. I knew I might have to go under the knife. "Smart thinking," he said. Then I remembered to ask him about the MRI results, just in case there was something abnormal. He checked and there wasn't. I was prepped for surgery.

My appendix was removed using minimally invasive surgery, and I felt great the next morning. The Dalles hospital has an incredible view of the river, and I sat drinking my tea thinking how good it felt to be pain free. The nurses joked about what a great patient I was and I went home that day.

Recovering the next day at home, I answered the phone. Dr. Moon asked me how I was feeling, how the incisions were, then told me my test results were back from pathology. "Do you want the good news or the bad news?" he asked.

"Oh, give me the bad news," I said, thinking, *How bad can it be?*

"There was a cancerous tumor in your appendix. We need to perform a right colectomy on you. It doesn't have to be tomorrow, but it should be by the end of the month."

What was the good news? I wondered. My husband was up at the shop, so I called and asked him to come down to the house. Then I told him the news. I set up an appointment to go in for consultation. I called my mom. I researched appendiceal cancer on the internet. I called a few girlfriends in shock and disbelief. One of them said, "See? You wished for time off and now you got it." Ouch. You learn which friends to go to for support.

I got second opinions and third opinions. They were identical. My type of tumor secretes mucous, and the surrounding intestine needed to be removed. I scheduled my surgery at the end of the month, after spring break. My nephew was graduating high school and I promised him a ski trip to Sun Valley.

I was scared. And bewildered. How could I have cancer? I ate right, exercised, and took supplements. I was a positive, optimistic person.

"I knew that flying would give you cancer," another friend said. I realized that cancer is so scary to so many people that they have to make up reasons why you got it and they didn't. Of course, most of my many friends were totally supportive, helpful, and wonderful. But you remember the weird comments.

My girlfriend shared her experience after being diagnosed with breast cancer. A religious neighbor told her she was lucky that God was taking her now, before the rapture and everything—that she was one of the chosen ones! That advice, needless to say, was not uplifting to her, either.

I spent the next few weeks preparing. I bought lounging pajamas and books to read, along with my favorite comfort foods. There were movies I wanted to watch, so I ordered those. This would be more of a fun, relaxing vacation.

The day of my surgery arrived. My gynecologist asked if he could observe, and I was flattered that he cared enough. Maybe it was just a surgery he hadn't seen before, but I welcomed his presence. The hospital offered a massage before surgery, and of course it was wonderful. You don't realize how much you are holding your breath and how tightly you are wound up. After all, this was a major operation and things could go wrong.

The next few days were a blur. I remember being in a private room. Then they moved me. I was on heavy morphine, but I do remember friends coming to visit. They moved me a couple more times. I hated changing rooms and feared getting a bad roommate.

I was in the hospital for a week, if that gives you any idea how serious this operation was in light of insurance and shortened hospital stays. The nurses didn't move me again because I had too many flowers and presents. I was thrilled. I had an amazing view of the Columbia Gorge. Being heavily sedated means you never get through a book, magazine, or conversation. It is too hard to track. Strangely, I enjoyed my hospital time. When you've spent your life in hotels, hospitals are not that different—except you have more company.

I was worried about going home. Spring work was keeping my husband busy. I was too weak and sore to fend well for myself. Luckily, it worked out. He worked at his shop most of the time, and would come down often to check on me. Friends stopped by with dinner and anything I needed.

It took a good six weeks to heal, but I still was nowhere close to being able to go back to work. I didn't have the stamina or the energy. Frankly, the thought of going back to work scared me. What if I only had three years to live? What if I had less? Did I want to spend any of that time away from my family? My answer was a definite no.

The decision was taken out of my hands. I had three more episodes of the visual headaches and was sent to a neurologist. She ran me through a barrage of tests, but found nothing neurologically wrong. The headaches were classified as visual migraines. I had a medication that knocked the symptoms down within twenty minutes. But the FAA said that if there was no warning before the headache, I couldn't fly.

I went on medical leave with Delta. My energy is coming back slowly. The fear that the cancer could resurface is less every day. I've learned how to say no to all but those things I want to do. Delta retired me at age sixty.

I flew all over the world in the best airplane ever made. All my dreams have come true, and I don't have anything to prove to anyone. I wake up every morning feeling blessed and grateful for all that I have. It sounds so weird to say that the cancer was a blessing, but to me it was. I never would have quit flying unless someone shot me out of the sky.

I can fly anything! (Photo by Bob Davis)

Next?

EPILOGUE

I am saddened to learn that the struggles and prejudices I experienced in my career still exist today. We will never reach a tipping point in this industry with numbers of women pilots hovering at 5%. There are thousands of women pilots who want nothing more than the stability and days off provided by a major airline. The majors are meeting the minimum numbers of minorities required by law: they are not striving for diversity.

I volunteer at Women in Aviation and I am the Communications Chair for the International Society of Women Airline Pilots, an organization that raises scholarship money for women whose career goal is to be an airline pilot. The stories I'm hearing of prejudice and harassment astound me. We early women pilots think we have made a difference, but it hasn't been enough.

ALPA, the pilot union, sees no reason to push for better family leave policies because women make up such a small percentage of their members. Women are afraid push for equality because what goes into their permanent records could affect their advancement and possible hiring at a legacy carrier. For example, each month of pregnancy leave is considered a separate absence at some regionals, and legacy carriers don't want to hire someone with more than two absences in a year! We have moved back into the dark ages... the stone age.

It will take a huge grass roots movement and some brave women to make a difference in this career.